M000313945

TABLE OF CONTENTS

APPENDICES

Internet Safety 101℠
Workbook & Resource Guide

Educate • Equip • Empower

ENOUGH·IS·ENOUGH
Making the Internet Safer for Children and Families

www.enough.org   www.internetsafety101.org

U.S. Department of Justice

Office of Justice Programs

Office of Juvenile Justice and Delinquency Prevention

Washington, D.C. 20531

October 7, 2009

Dear Internet Safety 101 curriculum recipient:

The Internet Safety 101 curriculum completes a multi-year effort by Enough Is Enough in partnership with the Office of Juvenile Justice and Delinquency Prevention (OJJDP) to create an educational program for parents, educators, and law enforcement to protect children from the threats they face across all Internet-enabled devices. Instead of leaving it to children and young people to learn how to protect themselves online, their parents, who must be the first line of defense, can better ensure that their children are safe and able to enjoy the many benefits the Internet has to offer. Furthermore, parents, educators and law enforcement representatives who are knowledgeable about online safety can better help children to take full advantage of Internet safety educational programs.

The 101 curriculum, which includes a DVD teaching series, accompanying workbook, and website, enhances OJJDP's current efforts to protect children from online victimization by offering parents, educators and law enforcement valuable information and resources about the dangers associated with Internet use, as well as steps they can take to reduce them. The four-part DVD is a comprehensive, "plug and play" program with on-screen instructors that harnesses the power of a live safety teaching without the need for trained facilitators. Another important feature of the 101 Program is that it can be used both by law enforcement officers trained in Internet safety and officers who may not have the same level of experience in this subject to expand education efforts in their communities.

Viewers will hear from noted experts in the field, learn of risks from technologies that are not often covered in other Internet safety programs, such as cell phones and gaming devices, and be educated about the entire spectrum of prevention efforts to protect children online. In fact, the Internet

Safety 101 curriculum actively promotes child-focused Internet safety initiatives that fall outside its purview, such as NetSmartz, Web Wise Kids, IKeepSafe and others. In addition, the curriculum includes interviews with young people about the dangers and benefits of the Internet in order to provide adults a clear understanding of what the Internet represents to the children and youth that use it.

It is the sincere hope of OJJDP that as parents, educators, law enforcement and children work together to increase their awareness of potential Internet dangers, the threats associated with those seeking to exploit Internet technology, and the safety solutions to protect children from such threats, fewer instances of online abuse and exploitation of children will result.

Sincerely,

Ron Laney
Associate Administrator
Child Protection Division
OJJDP

Industry

"By continuing to speak out and partner with the rest of the Internet, Donna Rice Hughes is helping all of us build a medium we can be proud of."

— Steve Case, former Chairman, American Online, Inc.

"Fox Interactive Media and MySpace.com are excited to work alongside Enough Is Enough (EIE) on the *Internet Safety 101*[SM] program. We commend your efforts as a pioneer and leader against Internet predators, as well as your innovative and effective educational programs. Thank you for all that you do in this important area of online safety."

— Hemanshu Nigam, Chief Security Officer, Fox Interactive Media and MySpace

"Enough Is Enough (EIE) has developed a unique approach to reach parents and adult childcare providers with the best resources and information on Internet safety, and we are aligned with EIE through our partnership for the *Internet Safety 101*[SM] program, which will ensure that parents receive the best information available about Internet safety concerns, resources and information."

— Brent M. Olson, Assistant Vice President, Regulatory Policy, AT&T

"Through the foresight and leadership of EIE, Internet Safety 101[SM] has established itself as the benchmark for all other Internet safety programs. The program was thoughtfully designed to educate and empower parents, teachers and guardians on Internet safety, and it was developed in a format that is accessible to everyone and is relevant to the dangers our children face online today."

— Steve F. Clementi, Director, Verizon External Affairs

"The program is a powerful tool as it is designed to educate the masses. Through the use of a segmented DVD and manual, parents and caregivers across the country will be able to benefit from EIE's teachings as well as the information given by industry leaders, health experts, and law enforcement officials. I have had the opportunity to participate in several Internet Safety presentations held by EIE in which segments of the Internet Safety 101[SM] program were shown and I have seen the positive impact that the program has had on parents."

— Holly M. Hawkins, Director, Policy & Regulatory, AOL, LLC

Media

"Donna is one of the leaders in the fight against pornography aimed at children on the Internet."

— **Oprah Winfrey**

"WMAL Radio is proud to support Enough Is Enough (EIE) and the Internet safety program you have created to protect children online. We are very excited about this new program and confident that it will present highly informative and useful information for all the families in our listening audience."

— **Ernest D. Fears, III, General Sales Manager, WMAL, News Talk 630**

"[Enough Is Enough] is an organization devoted to keeping online pornography off kids' computers."

— **Katie Couric,** *The Today Show*

"[Donna Rice Hughes] has been warning about the dangers for years. *Dateline* first spoke with her 11 years ago. But now, she says the problem has grown with the Internet giving predators accessibility, affordability, and the anonymity to feed their criminal acts."

— *Dateline* **NBC**

Parents

"The *Internet Safety 101*ᔆᴹ program represents the comprehensive, multi-media curriculum approach needed today to empower parents and the other adult child caregivers in Virginia with Internet safety rules and tools. It provides the 'take home' piece that will inform our parent and teacher members about why Internet child safety is such an important issue and equip and empower them to safeguard our children from these dangers at home and in our communities. We feel strongly that the *Internet Safety 101*ᔆᴹ program is a tailored-made response to the Internet child safety crisis facing our state and the nation. We are partnering with Enough Is Enough and applaud them for their contributions and tremendous service to parents, teachers, guadians, caregivers and all citizens of Virginia that will undoubtedly protect children throughout our Commonwealth."

— **Dianne Florence, Immediate Past President,
Virginia PTA & Melissa Nehrbass, President,
Virginia PTA**

"The Virginia Association of Independent Schools would like to commend Donna Rice Hughes and Enough Is Enough (EIE) for their tremendous work to make the Internet safer for children and families nationwide. EIE has developed a unique, grass-roots approach to reach parents and adult childcare providers with the best resources and information on Internet safety. The *Internet Safety 101*℠ program duplicates the important in-person training services that EIE has been providing for years."

— Sally K. Boese, Ed.D., Executive Director, Virginia Association of Independent Schools

"I attended your presentation and was very interested, and disturbed, to listen to the access and predatory practices related to the internet and youth that you relayed. I thought you may be interested to know that your presentation has sparked an interest and concern that may lead, at least one community to further addressing this problem."

— Parent & County Commissioner, Traverse City Michigan

"This Program is a real wake up call to parents who have been complacent!"

— Parent, Salt Lake City Utah

"It really opened my eyes about this kind of thing. I wish I had known more when my children were younger. Thank you for this program!"

— Parent, Salt Lake City Utah

"I truly enjoyed this [program]. I have learned a lot about Internet pornography, and every parent needs to hear and see this!"
"Best workshop of the conference!"
"Very informative and very helpful! Lots of good information!"

— Parent & *Internet Safety 101*℠ Workshop Participants, Eighth International Wesleyan Conference

"I have 12 grandchildren and love your organization."

— E. Winter

Organizations

"The Salvation Army is deeply concerned about online dangers facing children today, and has been working with Enough Is Enough for many years to deliver Internet safety training and information to the millions of families and parents we serve across the country. We commend Enough Is Enough for the development of the groundbreaking *Internet Safety 101*℠ program."

— **Major Ronald R. Foreman, ACSW, EJD, National Social Services Secretary, Salvation Army**

"EIE's preventative work motivates parents to establish proactive Internet safety rules and also to use the technological tools necessary to help prevent children from being victimized by online predators. At NCMEC, we have seen how every new technological innovation can be used for harm. Parents must remain informed to protect their children from this threat; EIE plays a critical role in educating parents to be involved in their children's online life, and I thank them for their tremendous work to protect children nationwide."

— **Ernie Allen, President & CEO, National Center for Missing and Exploited Children (NCMEC)**

"We are very excited about the Enough Is Enough *Internet Safety 101*℠ program, and its goal to educate parents and adult caregivers about Internet dangers and provide solutions to protect children online. The Internet safety training materials that EIE provides will alert and educate parents and adult caregivers about online sexual predators and pornographers who seek to victimize innocent and vulnerable children."

— **Kimberly Martinez, Executive Director, Abstinence Clearinghouse**

"The subject of Internet dangers is a serious issue for our families, and we are delighted to be able to bring Enough Is Enough's *Internet Safety 101*℠ program training to our members under [an AACC] educational series. The series has been a huge success and we thank you for everything you do to protect our families. We are very proud to be able to work with EIE on *Internet Safety 101*℠ in making the Internet a safer place for children and families everywhere."

— **Tim Clinton, President, American Association of Christian Counselors (AACC)**

Government & Law Enforcement

"EIE, headed by Donna Rice Hughes, has been a leading force in raising national recognition of the critically serious problem of Internet child pornography and sexual predation. EIE's *Internet Safety 101*ˢᴹ program educates parents comfortably, and I believe that EIE's *Internet Safety 101*ˢᴹ program [will] be a great asset for law enforcement and Project Safe Childhood task forces around the country in their community outreach efforts."

> **— Andrew G. Oosterbaan, Chief, U.S. Department of Justice,**
> **Criminal Division, Child Exploitation and Obscenity Section**

"Donna Rice Hughes is a strong and effective advocate for children's online safety."

> **— John Ashcroft, U.S. Attorney General (2001-2005)**

"As parents, we have the responsibility to monitor our children's use of the Internet. Ms. Hughes has presented us with a resource[1] to ensure that our children's experience using the Internet is a safe one."

> **— The Honorable Senator John McCain (AZ)**

"Enough Is Enough (EIE) is a significant partner, [and] EIE President Donna Rice Hughes has been a staunch proponent of parental education programs for Virginia. Through EIE's years of experience and work on this critical issue, and through EIE's singular work with parents nationwide, they are helping to shape the resources and tools that parents and educators across Virginia will receive. We are impressed with and endorse their comprehensive *Internet Safety 101*ˢᴹ concept."

> **— Lisa M. Hicks-Thomas, Deputy Attorney General, Virginia**

"I am pleased to have partnered with Enough Is Enough in the fight to keep our youth safe on the Internet. Their tireless efforts have produced this outstanding Internet Safety 101ˢᴹ Program. Parents will benefit greatly from this program and I am proud that our Office was able to contribute to its production.

> **— Robert F. McDonnell, Former Attorney General of Virginia**

"The Enough is Enough curriculum for parents, teachers, and caring adults is the most thorough information and training of its type available to those who want to protect their families from predators and pornographers. Donna Rice Hughes, Enough is Enough President, takes the viewer on a necessary trip that covers not only computer risks, but the dangers that a young person can encounter from cyber bullying, cell phones, and social networking. It might be called Internet Safety 101ˢᴹ, but it's really a graduate course for those who don't want to watch their child heal after abuse, but keep them safe in the first place."

> **— Robert J. Flores, Esq., Former Administrator of the Office of Juvenile Justice**
> **and Delinquency Prevention, U.S. Department of Justice**

[1] Sen. John McCain was commenting on EIE President Donna Rice Hughes's book <u>Kids Online</u>, Published By Fleming H. Revell, a division of Baker Book House Company, 1998.

About Us

Enough Is Enough (EIE), a non-partisan, 501(c)(3) non-profit organization, emerged in 1994 as the national leader on the front lines to make the Internet safer for children and families. Since then, EIE has pioneered efforts to confront online pornography, child pornography, child stalking, sexual predation, and other forms of online victimization. By leveraging its expertise, growing national partnership network, and positive reputation among the public, media, law enforcement, and Internet industry, EIE continues to advance innovative initiatives and effective communication strategies to protect children online.

Mission Statement

The **Enough Is Enough** mission is to *Make the Internet Safer for Children and Families*. EIE is dedicated to continuing to raise public awareness about online dangers, specifically the dangers of Internet pornography and sexual predators. EIE advances solutions that promote equality, fairness, and respect for human dignity with shared responsibility between the public, technology, and the law. EIE stands for freedom of speech as defined by the Constitution of the United States; for a culture where all people are respected and valued; for a childhood with a protected age of innocence; for healthy sexuality; and, for a society free from sexual exploitation.

The Problem

Despite its tremendous benefits, the Internet has opened the door for predators to sexually exploit unsuspecting children and allows obscenely graphic and addictive pornography to lurk only a mouse click away from innocent youth. The Internet has also fostered an environment for new threats including cyberbullying and identity theft. Unfortunately, parents and other adults are uninformed and ill-equipped to deal with evolving issues of Internet safety and need credible outside help.

The Solution

EIE has a three-pronged, preventative approach to create and sustain a safe, entertaining, and informative Internet environment, free from sexual predators, the intrusion of unwanted sexual material, and other harmful and exploitative online threats by:

Education: Raising public awareness of the threat of illegal pornography, sexual predation, and other Internet dangers in order to empower and equip parents and other child caregivers to implement safety measures;

Industry: Encouraging the technology industry to implement viable technological solutions and family-friendly corporate policy to reduce online threats; and,

Enforcement: Promoting legal solutions by calling for aggressive enforcement of existing laws and enactment of new laws to stop the exploitation and victimization of children using the Internet.

In September 2005, EIE received support from the Office of Juvenile Justice and Delinquency Prevention, U.S. Department of Justice, and other partners to begin a new program—*Internet Safety 101*^{SM}—to educate and empower parents, guardians, and other adult caregivers to implement Internet safety rules and software tools *(Rules 'N Tools®)* and provide communities with information and resources to support local action to markedly increase the safety of children online.

Special Acknowledgments

Enough Is Enough would like to thank all those who provided their expertise, testimony, time, energy, and talent to help make *Internet Safety 101*℠ a comprehensive and valuable resource to educate, empower, and equip parents everywhere to protect their children online. This program is dedicated to the children across this country: ***Your innocence is worth fighting for!***

These efforts would not have been possible without the support of our Founding Circle Sponsors, Partners and other Supporting Organizations, who stood with us from the beginning!

Founding Circle Sponsors

Anschutz Foundation

AOL

AT&T

Fieldstead & Company

Fox Interactive Media

MDRT Foundation

MySpace

Office of Juvenile Justice and Delinquency Prevention (OJJDP)

Shelby Collum Davis Foundation

Verizon

Wiebe Foundation

Program Partners & Other Supporting Organizations

Ad Council

American Association of Christian Counselors

Atlantic Video

Bonnemaison Inc.

Center for Safe and Responsible Internet Use

Christian Broadcasting Network

Clear Channel

Coker Logistics Solutions

CR-18 Child Exploitation Squad, FBI

e-Copernicus

EIE Internet Safety Council

GetNetWise

House of Hope Orlando

iKeepSafe

Klarquist Sparkman, LLP

Lighted Candle Society

McLean Bible Church

National Center for Missing and Exploited Children

National District Attorneys Association

National Organization of Black Law Enforcement Executives

NetSmartz411

Office of the Virginia Attorney General

Progress and Freedom Foundation

Sheriff Mike Brown, Bedford County, VA ICAC

TechMission

The Salvation Army

U.S. District Attorney's Office, Western PA

Virginia PTA

WAVA Radio

Web Wise Kids

WMAL Radio

Special Acknowledgments

Enough Is Enough Personnel

(*indicates past personnel)

Byron Bartlett

Coraleen Braxton*

Diane Brown

Robert J. Flores, Esq.[1]

Cris Clapp Logan

Meredith Connell*

Kathy Hatem*

Donna Rice Hughes

Dona Jones*

Steve Kussmann*

Lillian Schoeppler

Judy Wong*

[1] Special Counsel to EIE President and Former Administrator of the Office of Juvenile Justice and Delinquency Prevention, U.S. Department of Justice.

Enough Is Enough's Internet Safety Council

Stephen Balkam, CEO, Family Online Safety Institute

Mary Beth Buchanan, U.S. District Attorney, PA

James Dirksen, RuleSpace

Dianne Florence, Former President, Virginia PTA

Rebecca Hagelin, Former Vice President, Communications & Marketing, Heritage Foundation

Michael J. Harmony, Lieutenant, Bedford County, VA, Sheriff's Office, Special Investigation Division

Holly Hawkins, Director of Policy & Regulatory, Consumer Advocacy, AOL LLC

Major Betty Israel, National Social Service Secretary, Salvation Army

Alicia & Mary Kozakiewicz

Jill C. Manning, Ph.D., LMFT

Rick Minicucci, Former President of NetSmartz, CTO of NCMEC

Melissa Nehrbass, President, Virginia PTA

Tony Nassif, Cedars Cultural and Educational Foundation

Hemanshu Nigam, Chief Security Officer, Fox Interactive Media and MySpace

Wayne S. Promisel, Child Welfare League of America, Juvenile Justice Division

Judith A. Reisman, Ph.D.

Rene, Mother of an Internet Pornography Victim

Adam Thierer, Senior Fellow & Director, Progress and Freedom Foundation's Center for Digital Media Freedom (CDMF)

James B. Weaver, III, Ph.D.

Judi Westberg-Warren, President, Web Wise Kids

Nancy Willard, Director, Center for Safe and Responsible Internet Use

Virginia PTA Internet Safety Task Force

Marion Akins

Anne Carson

Dianne Florence

Debbie Kilpatrick

Melissa Nehrbass

Dan Phillips

Sherri Wright

EIE Board of Directors

Donna Rice Hughes
Chairman

Commissioner Eva Gaither
National President of Women's Ministries for The Salvation Army in the United States of America

Colby M. May
Senior Counsel & Director of the ACLJ Washington Office

Mark Larson
News Radio San Diego 1700AM

EIE Advisory Board

Mark E. Gilman
Decus Communication

Rebecca Hagelin
Former Vice President, Communications & Marketing, Heritage Foundation

Jack Hughes
Founder & Principal, Phoenix Financial Advisory Services

Dee Jepsen
President Emeritus, Enough Is Enough

Gayle Miller
Former Anne Klein President

Bud Moeller
Former Vice President for Booz, Allen & Hamilton; Partner at Accenture

Pam Pryor
Former Vice President of Government Relations for We Care America

Kevin Reynolds
President of Cardinal Bank

Pat Roddy
Award-Winning Television and Film Producer

Mike Schick
Partner, Adfero Group

Ruth Sims
Marketing and Development Strategist and Consultant

Special Thanks

Enough Is Enough wishes to thank the production company of Bonnemaison Inc. for their invaluable contributions to the making of the *Internet Safety 101*^{SM} DVD series. The success of this program is due in no small measure to their talented team of producers, directors, writers, and editors. Their dedication, sacrifice, and commitment to excellence made this program possible.

Internet Safety 101^{SM} **Workbook**

Writers & Editors:

Cris Clapp Logan

Kathy Hatem

Donna Rice Hughes

Nina Seebeck

Legal Counsel:

Ray Klitzke II
Klarquist Sparkman, LLP

Colby May
American Center for Law and Justice

Workbook Art Direction and Design:

Sean Mullins

Additional Designers:

Mike Bloom

Kris Jenkins (cover photos)

Nicole Kassolis

Bill Santry (laptop Kit)

Theresa Wallace

Biography

Donna Rice Hughes
President and Chairman

Donna Rice Hughes, President and Chairman of Enough Is Enough (EIE), is an internationally known Internet safety expert, author, and speaker. As a respected leader of national efforts to protect children online, Donna has championed EIE's mission to make the Internet safer for children and families since 1994. Under her leadership and vision, EIE created the *Internet Safety 101*℠ program with the U.S. Department of Justice and other partners. She is also the executive producer, host, and instructor of the *Internet Safety 101*℠ DVD series, the cornerstone element of the *101* program.

Donna is frequently sought out by educators, policy makers, law enforcement officials, and industry leaders for her Internet safety expertise, and she has been a featured guest and Internet safety expert on leading national broadcasts including *Dateline*, *The Today Show*, *The O'Reilly Factor*, *Oprah* and *20/20*. Donna has given more than 3,500 media interviews and has been a regular commentator on Internet safety issues on CNN, Fox News, and MSNBC. Her views and editorials have been featured in *The Wall Street Journal*, *The New York Times*, *The Washington Post*, *USA Today*, *The San Francisco Chronicle*, *The San Jose Mercury News*, *The Los Angeles Times*, *The Philadelphia Inquirer*, *People* magazine, and *McCall's* magazine. Donna was described as "one of the leaders in the fight against pornography aimed at children" by Oprah Winfrey, and applauded as a pioneer on Internet safety, "helping all of us build a medium we can be proud of," by Steve Case, founder of America Online.

She co-wrote the story for the May 2000 season finale episode of *Touched By An Angel* that brought the message of Internet dangers and online safety to prime time television and won the Nielsen ratings for its time slot during the May sweeps period. Her book, *Kids Online: Protecting Your Children In Cyberspace* (Revell, September 1998), was heralded worldwide and has been translated into Spanish and Korean.

Donna has spoken extensively on the subject of Internet safety in educational and professional forums nationwide, offering her expert advice to parents, legislators, law enforcement officials, and industry leaders on ways to protect vulnerable children.

Donna has testified numerous times before the United States Congress on Internet dangers and safety solutions. Her seminar at the Department of Justice's Federal Prosecutors' Obscenity Symposium was applauded as a "highlight" of the 2002 meeting by Andrew Oosterbaan, chief of the Child Exploitation and Obscenity Section, where Donna served as the Department's only non-lawyer/non-law enforcement instructor.

Donna was appointed by Senator Trent Lott to serve on the Child Online Protection Act (COPA, 1998) Commission and served as co-chair of the COPA Hearings on filtering/ratings/labeling technologies. She also serves on various Internet safety advisory boards and task forces including the 2006 Virginia Attorney General's Youth Internet Safety Task Force and the 2008 Internet Safety Technical Task Force, formed with MySpace and the U.S. Attorneys General.

Donna has received numerous awards including the National Law Center for Children and Families Annual Appreciation Award, and the "Protector of Children Award" and Media Impact Award from the National Abstinence Clearinghouse.

Donna received a Bachelor of Science degree from the University of South Carolina and graduated Magna Cum Laude and Phi Beta Kappa. She is married to Jack Hughes and has two grown step-children, Sean and Mindy, and a grandson, Alexander Briggs.

Internet Safety 101^{SM}
Subject Experts and Featured Guests

Ernie Allen

Ernie Allen is the President & CEO of the National Center for Missing and Exploited Children (NCMEC) and the International Centre for Missing and Exploited Children (ICMEC). Through his leadership, NCMEC has played a role in the recovery of 74,000 children, with NCMEC's recovery rate climbing from 62% in 1990 to 94% today. He has also taken NCMEC's programs and services to a global audience, including the building of a missing children's network that includes 14 nations.

W. Dean Belnap, M.D.

Dr. Belnap is a Fellow of the American Academy of Pediatrics and a Fellow in the American Psychiatric Association. He has been on the Primary Children's Hospital staff for 46 years and is an Emeritus Clinical Professor of Psychiatry at the University of Utah. He has been Medical Director at Valley Mental Health: ARTEC Unit, Medical Director of Rivendell of America, and a President Reagan appointee to the Advisory Council of Health and Human Services. He has written several books about children with behavioral problems and neurological difficulties, continues to serve as a pediatrician and child and adolescent psychiatrist, and is a member of the Society for Behavioral Pediatrics.

Mary Beth Buchanan

Mary Beth Buchanan is the United States Attorney for the Western District of Pennsylvania. Ms. Buchanan oversees the prosecution of all federal crimes, and the litigation of civil matters in which the federal government has an interest, throughout the 25 counties in western Pennsylvania. From November 2006 through December 2007, Ms. Buchanan served as the Acting Director for the Department of Justice's Office on Violence Against Women. Between April 2003 and May 2004, Ms. Buchanan served as chair of Attorney General John Ashcroft's Advisory Committee of United States Attorneys. This committee counsels the Attorney General on law enforcement issues and plays an integral role in setting Department of Justice policy. Ms. Buchanan also serves on Enough Is Enough's Internet Safety Council.

Cris Clapp Logan

Cris Logan joined the Enough Is Enough (EIE) team in 2007 as Congressional Liaison and Research Analyst. In her work with EIE, she educates congressional staff on Internet safety issues and handles communications-related issues for the organization. Mrs. Logan also manages media inquiries for EIE and contributes regularly on national radio and to print publications. She works closely with EIE President Donna Rice Hughes to advance EIE's initiatives with public, industry, and law enforcement efforts, participating with the Virginia Attorney General's *Youth Internet Safety Task Force*, the GetNetWise Advisory Board, and the *Internet Safety Technical Task Force*, on behalf of Mrs. Hughes. Mrs. Logan also serves on the *TIP & Technology: Uses and Abuses of Technology in Human Trafficking Roundtable*, U.S. Department of State. Mrs. Logan speaks at conferences in areas relating to Internet pornography, teen web identity, and the Web 2.0.

Chad Gallagher

Chad Gallagher is a Special Agent with the Child Exploitation Squad at the FBI's Washington Field Office. This squad handles all crimes against children, including the online sexual exploitation of children, the commercial sexual exploitation of children, and child abductions. Mr. Gallagher specializes in online child exploitation investigations using multiple technology platforms, including multiplayer online gaming communities.

Holly Hawkins

Holly Hawkins is the Director of Policy & Regulatory for AOL, LLC. Holly has over a decade of experience in forging best practices for AOL in the area of kids and teen protection. Holly is responsible for a wide range of consumer protection and risk management issues for AOL's brands including child privacy and safety, content, and community standards as well as product moderation and enforcement standards. Ms. Hawkins serves on Enough Is Enough's Internet Safety Council.

Justin Hart

Justin Hart is the Vice President of Communications for The Lighted Candle Society, a nationwide community of concerned citizens dedicated to the eradication of pornography. The Lighted Candle Society supports civil litigation against those that profit from pornography, finances scientific research to study the effects of pornography, and publishes information to help families combat the scourge of pornography.

Sergeant Morani M. Hines

Morani M. Hines is the Detective Sergeant of the Child Exploitation Task Force with the Metropolitan Police Department in Washington, D.C., whose mission is to combat child sexual exploitation. Sergeant Hines also works with the Crimes Against Children Unit at the FBI's Washington Field Office.

Alicia Kozakiewicz

Alicia Kozakiewicz is a teen survivor of an Internet predator. At the age of 13, she was abducted from her family home by someone she had met online. For four days, she was tortured and held captive in the basement of her abductor. Now, as a student at Pittsburgh University, Alicia has continued her mission to educate children and families on the dangers of the Internet by sharing her story. Alicia is a member of Enough Is Enough's Internet Safety Council, and has appeared in Internet safety films for the FBI and the Pennsylvania Center for Safe Schools. In 2007, she received the National Center for Missing and Exploited Children's Courage Award. A key legislative initiative, "Alicia's Law," has been launched in her name throughout the country to increase funding for the Internet Crimes Against Children Task Force officers on the front lines of tracking cyber predators.

Mary Kozakiewicz

Mary Kozakiewicz is the mother of Alicia Kozakiewicz, a teen survivor of an Internet predator. She is a member of Team HOPE, which is dedicated to empowering the families of missing children, as well as the "Surviving Parents Coalition," an organization consisting of parents whose children had been abducted and abused. She advances initiatives to increase funding for programs dedicated to protecting children online and advocates for increased funding for Internet Crimes Against Children Task Forces. She is also a member of Enough Is Enough's Internet Safety Council.

Subject Experts and Featured Guests

Jonathan Larcomb

Jonathan Larcomb is a prosecutor and Assistant Attorney General II for the Computer Crimes Section of the Attorney General's Office in Richmond, Virginia. In addition to prosecuting child exploitation cases in state and federal court, he travels throughout Virginia educating students, parents, and community groups on Internet safety.

Tim Lordan

Tim Lordan is the Executive Director of the Internet Education Foundation, a non-partisan, non-profit 501(c)(3) organization, dedicated to educating the public and policy makers about the potential of a decentralized global Internet to promote democracy, communications, and commerce. Mr. Lordan is also the Executive Director of GetNetWise, a public service to help ensure that Internet users have safe, constructive, and educational or entertaining online experiences, where he helped develop and launch the GetNetWise one-click parental empowerment resource.

Jill C. Manning, Ph.D.

Dr. Jill C. Manning is a Licensed Marriage and Family Therapist who specializes in clinical work related to pornography use and compulsive sexual behavior. She recently authored a book titled *What's the Big Deal about Pornography?: A Guide for the Internet Generation*. The purpose of her book is to provide young adults, parents, and youth leaders valuable information about the harms of pornography and resources for overcoming its influence. Dr. Manning also serves on Enough Is Enough's Internet Safety Council.

Melissa Morrow

Melissa Morrow is the Supervisory Special Agent of the Child Exploitation Squad at the FBI's Washington Field Office. This squad handles all crimes against children, including the online sexual exploitation of children, the commercial sexual exploitation of children, and child abductions. Members of this squad are also part of a Child Exploitation Task Force with the Metropolitan Police Department in Washington, D.C., whose mission is to combat the sexual exploitation of children.

Hemanshu Nigam

Hemanshu Nigam serves as the first Chief Security Officer for News Corp.'s Internet division, and Senior Vice President for Fox Interactive Media (FIM), where he oversees all safety, security, education, privacy, and law enforcement programs for MySpace and other FIM properties. A veteran in online security, Nigam brings more than 18 years of experience in both private industry and law enforcement fields. He has previously served as a federal prosecutor against Internet child exploitation and computer crimes for the U.S. Department of Justice, as an advisor to a congressional commission on online child safety, and an advisor to the White House on cyberstalking. He also served in various strategic roles inside Microsoft Corporation. Nigam serves as a member of the Board of the Family Online Safety Institute (FOSI) and of the Internet Safety Council of Enough is Enough.

Judith Reisman, Ph.D.

Dr. Judith Reisman is a Cultural Trend Analyst and Human Sexuality Researcher. Dr. Reisman's research has analyzed how sexually explicit materials have shaped individual thinking, behavior, and social contagion. Dr. Reisman is president of The Institute for Media Education, author of the U.S. Department of Justice, Juvenile Justice study, *Images of Children, Crime and Violence in Playboy, Penthouse and Hustler (1989); Kinsey, Sex and Fraud (Reisman, et al., 1990); Soft Porn Plays Hardball (1991);* and *Kinsey, Crimes & Consequences (1998, 2000)*. She has been a consultant to four U.S. Department of Justice administrations, The U.S. Department of Education, as well as the U.S. Department of Health and Human Services. Dr. Reisman serves on Enough Is Enough's Internet Safety Council.

Nancy E. Willard

Nancy Willard is the Director of the Center for Safe and Responsible Internet Use. She frequently lectures and conducts workshops for educators on policies and practices related to Internet use in schools and has written numerous articles on this subject. She is also author of *Cyberbullying and Cyberthreats: Responding to the Challenges of Online Social Aggression, Threats, and Distress* and *Cyber-Safe Kids & Cyber-Savvy Teens: Helping Young People Learn to Use the Internet Safely and Responsibly*. She educates parents, children, and educators on cyberbullying and Internet safety. Ms. Willard serves on Enough Is Enough's Internet Safety Council.

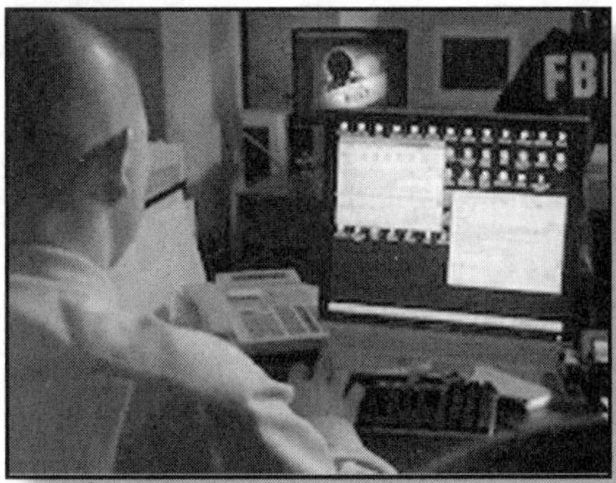

FBI Undercover Agents

Enough Is Enough (EIE) had the privilege of interviewing several undercover agents, whose faces and names could not be included in our production. These heroic men and women are on the front lines of the battle to save children from online exploitation, and they are exposed to some of the most horrific content and conduct imaginable. Their tireless work comes at great sacrifice, but it is by their sacrifice and dedication to protecting children that those who seek to violate our children's innocence are brought to justice. Their interviews and advice have provided key information for the *Internet Safety 101*℠ program.

Left to right, back: Kelly, Caroline, Allie;
Left to right, front: Meghan, Courtney

Also Featured
Youth Testimonials

Enough Is Enough (EIE) spoke with children, teens, and parents about their Internet experiences, and we are grateful for their participation in the *Internet Safety 101*℠ program. Each child and teen interviewed expressed their hope that their testimony would help educate parents about the benefits and dangers they encountered online; each demonstrated a distinct level of honesty, vulnerability, and humor, providing an invaluable contribution to this program.

Left to right, back: Sarah Trollinger, Donna Rice Hughes; Left to right, middle: Augey, Zach, Aaron; Left to right, front: Justin, Kyle, Dustin

Left to right: Sahmir, Dionte, Grant, KJ

"Rene"

As a mother of a victim of pornography addiction, "Rene" brings a special perspective to the *Internet Safety 101*^{SM} program. Because of her personal experience with the pervasive nature and detrimental effects of Internet pornography, she is dedicated to helping others avoid such trauma. Rene is also an Adjunct Professor of Law; she has served in multiple legal and advisory roles throughout the state of Virginia. She serves her community in many ways and is an active speaker to groups on cancer education and awareness.

"John Doe"

In the spring of 2008, Enough Is Enough President Donna Rice Hughes and a film crew interviewed convicted sex offender "John Doe" under the condition of anonymity. The interview was granted by the office of the Virginia Attorney General, and interview excerpts are included to educate parents about the modus operandi of Internet predators and to empower them to protect their children from victimization. The former elementary teacher is serving out his sentence after pleading guilty to forcible sodomy, production of child pornography, and online solicitation of children.

Internet Safety 101℠ In the Making

Introduction

Thank you for joining our efforts to make the Internet safer for children and families! Since 1994, Enough Is Enough (EIE) has been on the front lines of efforts to protect children online. Year after year, one thing remains constant: parental involvement is the key to protecting kids online! Whether you're a parent, grandparent, guardian, or educator, the goal of this series is to educate, empower, and equip you with regard to Internet dangers so that the children under your care can enjoy the many benefits the Internet has to offer.

When I was a child, every day held a new outdoor adventure, and being stuck inside felt like a fate worse than death! My sister and I rode our bikes until the sun set and used lightning bug-filled jars and moonlight to illuminate our nighttime games. We could roam freely around the neighborhood as long as we were not late for supper. Twig-induced scrapes and errant fishing hooks comprised our parents' major safety concerns, and our only "screen-time" was on our 12-inch family TV.

Back then, life was simple, carefree, and innocent; the world depicted on one of my favorite cartoons, *The Jetsons*, seemed like an illusive fantasy. Times have certainly changed (apart from the flying cars) and what was once yesterday's futuristic fantasy has become today's lifestyle. *This is* the digital age: *this is cyberspace*. And *this* is the world our children are growing up in.

As with any technology, although the Internet itself is neutral, it can be used for tremendous good or tremendous evil. At the click of a mouse, we can deliver important information or spread damaging gossip to hundreds of people. As new grandparents, my husband, Jack, and I have been thrilled to use webcam technology to see and hear our beautiful grandson as he grows, "coos," and cries, in *real time*, from *3,000 miles away!* Unfortunately, we have also seen how pedophiles around the globe can use this same technology to view the real-time molestation of innocent children. The amazing power of the Internet has been hijacked and used to invade the age of innocence every child deserves.

The Perfect Storm

Over the past fifteen years, a number of dynamic, powerful, and destructive elements have come together, creating a "perfect storm" scenario for our children to fall victim to exploitation in the digital age.

For the first time, sexual predators can communicate with unparalleled and anonymous access with our children, violating the safe walls of our homes, without our knowledge. There are over 644,865 registered sex offenders in the United States, and over 100,000 have been lost in the system.[2]

The Internet has also become the leading technology for distributing hard-core pornography, grossing $13 billion annually. Internet child pornography is a $3 billion per-year industry, and sadly, this horrific abuse represents one of the fastest growing businesses online. Everyone—including your child—is potentially one click away from having a virtual sexual interaction or being exposed to material once only available on the black market.

Almost 93% of kids, ages 12-17, are online,[3] and most exhibit a level of digital proficiency bewildering to those of us who want to protect them. Kids are feeling pressured to post provocative pictures, videos, and blog about their deepest personal experiences in a very public forum. Without guidance from parents and educators, few are thinking through the implications of their online actions.

To make matters worse, many of the legal measures we need to protect kids on our virtual streets are unenforced or outdated, and law enforcement and prosecutorial efforts are often underfunded.

Significant gaps exist between the Internet's dangers to children and the level of legal, enforcement-based, and industry-driven action dedicated to protecting children. In this ever-changing world, parents must stand in the gap and be the *'first line of defense'* against child Internet victimization. The challenge is that children are the *"digital natives,"* and parents are the *"digital immigrants."* Children are "native speakers" of the digital language of computers, video games, and the Internet, and many parents have not been able to develop digital proficiency.[4] Parents are often left feeling overwhelmed, uninformed, or ill-equipped to adequately protect their kids online.

> A **perfect storm** results when a number of powerful and dynamic events occur simultaneously. Such occurrences are rare by their very nature, so that even a slight change in any one event contributing to the perfect storm would lessen its overall impact.

[2] State or Territory Sex Offender Registries States and PR: U.S. Census Bureau, July 2006. Estimates Territories: Central Intelligence Agency, World Fact Book, July 2007 Estimates National Center for Missing & Exploited Children (NCMEC), Alexandria, VA, Environmental Systems Research Institute (ESRI), Inc., Redlands, CA.

[3] Lenhart, Amanda and Mary Madden. Teens, Privacy, and Online Social Networks. Pew Internet and American Life Project, 18 Apr. 2007.

[4] Prensky, Marc. "Digital Natives, Digital Immigrants." From On the Horizon (MCB University Press, Vol. 9 No. 5, October 2001) © 2001 Marc Prensky.

Introduction

Standing in the Gap

The good news is that you don't need a Ph.D. in digital technologies to protect your children in these dangerous waters. Studies continue to demonstrate that kids whose parents simply talk to them about Internet safety display significantly safer online behaviors; they are less likely to look at inappropriate content, talk to strangers, and experience cyberbullying while online.

Over the years we have seen that, although the content and the capabilities of the Internet have evolved, the basics you need to know to keep kids safe in this ever-evolving digital world continue to hold true. Although kids are now at risk of encountering inappropriate content and dangerous people across multiple platforms, the basic modus operandi utilized online by the pornography industry and sexual predators has not significantly changed. Even more promising: the basics of Internet safety have not changed significantly, either. It's upon these fundamental Internet safety principles—basic safety rules and software tools

(*Rules 'N Tools®*)—that we have built our national reputation for effective Internet safety education.

As the national demand for effective Internet safety seminars continued to grow, we began developing a unique program to deliver the power of our in-person seminars with the reach achievable only through the duplicative power of a multi-media production; hence, the *Internet Safety 101*^{SM} program was birthed.

Internet Safety 101^{SM}

The *Internet Safety 101*^{SM} program brings the experts to you. *Internet Safety 101*^{SM} combines the most critical Internet safety information with testimony, advice, and information from the leading experts, delivering comprehensive Internet safety solutions directly into the homes and hands of parents, educators, and guardians nationwide.

Throughout the production of the DVD teaching series, we have had the pleasure of working first-hand with the nation's leading law enforcement officials, policy shapers, industry visionaries, child victimization researchers, practitioners, clinicians, and psychologists, as well as those who have fallen victim to online exploitation: each has played a crucial role in the development of this resource.

This compelling, all-inclusive DVD series and accompanying workbook will teach you how to apply key safety principles across all Internet-enabled platforms used by your children. *Internet Safety 101*^{SM} also points parents toward the best websites and organizational resources for specific, topical, and child-focused solutions. Whether you and your spouse gather around your home television, or hundreds of concerned parents convene in a convention center, groups of any size can view this Internet safety film series simply by pressing "play" on a DVD player.

The multi-media teaching series is designed for flexibility, and each of the first three segments of the DVD (*Pornography 101*, *Predators 101*, and *The Evolving Internet: Web 2.0*) can be viewed separately or in combination with the *Safety 101* segment, and participants can follow along in the corresponding workbook segments. Additional information and partner tutorials are also included in the Special Features section of the DVD and in the workbook appendices. Each workbook segment also includes a narrative section ("A Closer Look"), which provides additional information, as well as victim testimonials, advice from featured experts, discussion questions, compelling statistics, and quizzes relating to each segment.

As parents, grandparents, and educators, we all long for our children to experience the childhood freedoms and protected age of innocence that touched our formative years. Once you complete the *Internet Safety 101*℠ program, we hope that you will be encouraged and equipped to protect your children more effectively on the Internet, affording them a safe and rewarding experience online, and ensuring a protected age of innocence for the children under your care.

We have been overwhelmed with the outpouring of support and encouragement from the parents, educators, and experts who have viewed each element of this production as it has come together. As any one of them would tell you: be prepared to laugh, cry, and become motivated to take those first critical steps along the path toward protecting your children online.

The entire Enough Is Enough team has worked tirelessly over the past year to develop this program. It has been a labor of love from our heart to yours, and we are thrilled that you are participating. *Thank you* for allowing us to help you protect your children online. Together, we can make a difference.

Let's get started!

For the Sake of the Children,

Donna Rice Hughes

Donna Rice Hughes

President and Chairman, Enough Is Enough

SEGMENT 1
PORNOGRAPHY 101

Introduction

Pornography has become increasingly acceptable, accessible, and freely available, and it is one of the biggest threats to our children's online safety. Today, any computer-literate child can view, either intentionally or accidentally, sexually explicit material online, from adult pornography (the kind of images that appear in *Playboy*) to prosecutable material depicting graphic sex acts, live sex shows, orgies, bestiality, and violence. Even material depicting the actual sexual abuse of a child (child pornography) that was once only found on the black market is instantly available and accessible on the Internet.

Most pornography sites offer free introductory viewing (teaser images) in an attempt to entice viewers, whet their appetites, and eventually secure paying customers. Everyone (including our children!) is just **a mouse click away** from having an anonymous, private, virtual sexual interaction.

"In 1993, when the Internet became public, there was this huge shift culturally; that protective barrier between the sex industry and youth dissolved. There used to be restricted movie houses, order catalogues with brown paper [wrappers] that came in the mail; things which a youth had a difficult time accessing. Now, through the Internet, you have pornography in your home. And so, that protective barrier just dissolved."

♀ Jill Manning, Ph.D.
Marriage and Family Therapist

SEGMENT 1 GOALS:

TO TEACH YOU ABOUT:
- ✔ The types of pornography online;
- ✔ The way Internet pornographers operate;
- ✔ How pornography impacts children; and
- ✔ Warning signs and rules of engagement.

What Is Pornography?[1]

Pornography can be thought of as all sexually explicit material intended primarily to arouse the reader, viewer, or listener. Each category of pornography has a specific legal definition established by the courts. The United States Supreme Court has said that there are four categories of pornography that can be determined illegal, which include: indecency, material harmful to minors, obscenity, and child pornography.

A) Indecent material includes messages or pictures on telephone, radio, or broadcast TV that are patently offensive descriptions or depictions of sexual or excretory organs or activities. It is often referred to as "sexual nudity" and "dirty words."

B) Material harmful to minors (HTM) represents nudity or sex that has prurient appeal for minors, is offensive and unsuitable for minors, and lacks serious value for minors. There are "harmful to minors" laws in every state.

 Note: Indecent and harmful to minors material (often referred to as "soft-core pornography") is legal for adults but illegal when knowingly sold or exhibited to minors (children under the age of 18). There is currently no federal indecency or harmful to minors statute that applies to the Internet! Two such measures have been passed by Congress and signed into law—the Communications Decency Act (CDA) in 1996, and the Child Online Protection Act (COPA) in 1998. The CDA indecency provision was struck down by the Supreme Court in 1997. Since COPA was passed in 1998, it has been held up in the courts and has therefore never gone into effect.

◯➤ EXAMPLES OF INDECENCY/HARMFUL TO MINORS:

_____

_____

EXAMPLES OF INDECENCY/HARMFUL
TO MINORS
ANSWERS:
Playboy magazine
Penthouse magazine

Sex & Pornography ■ Has Access ☐ Does Not Have Access

DESCRIPTION	PRINT		BROADCAST		CABLE		VIDEO & PPV		INTERNET	
	ADULTS	CHILDREN	ADULTS	CHILDREN	ADULTS	CHILDREN	ADULTS	CHILDREN	ADULTS	CHILDREN
Soft-core/HTM	Yes	No	No	No	Yes	No	Yes	No	Yes	Yes
Hard-core/Obscenity	Yes	No	No	No	No	No	Yes	No	Yes	Yes
Child Pornography	No	No	No	No	No	No	No	No	Yes	Yes

C) Obscenity ("hard-core pornography") is graphic

material that focuses on sex and/or sexual violence. It includes close-ups of graphic sex acts, lewd exhibition of the genitals, and deviant activities such as group sex, bestiality, torture, incest, and excretory functions.

The 1973 Supreme Court case of *Miller v. California* resulted in a clear, concise definition of obscenity (material that is prurient, patently offensive, and lacking in serious value). The Miller test is the United States Supreme Court's test for determining whether speech or expression can be labeled "obscene," in which case it is not protected by the First Amendment to the United States Constitution and can be prohibited.

 There are federal obscenity laws that criminalize distribution of obscenity on the Internet, but they have not been vigorously enforced.

D) Child pornography is material that visually depicts chil-

dren under the age of 18 engaged in actual or simulated sexual activity, including lewd exhibition of the genitals.

 Laws dealing with child pornography on the Internet are being aggressively enforced in the United States, but the problem appears to be larger than state or federal law enforcement can control. It is <u>illegal</u> to produce, distribute, or possess child pornography in the United States!

[1] Definitions excerpted in part from Rice Hughes, Donna, and Pamela Campbell. <u>Kids Online: Protecting Your Children in Cyberspace</u>. Michigan: Revell, 1998.

Question:

Why do parents need to be more vigilant about protecting their kids from all types of pornography in the online world as opposed to pornography in print, video, and broadcast?

Answer:

Children do not have the same protection from pornography in the online world as they do in the offline world.

Did You Know...

Pornography can also be accessed using the following devices:

- **Mobile Devices**
  (cell phones, PDAs)
- **MP3 Players**
  (iPods)
- **Gaming Devices**
  (PlayStation, Xbox, etc.)

News Stat

As mobile subscribers become more comfortable and familiar with the off-portal environment, **the traffic to these sites is likely to mushroom.** The increasing adoption of streamed video and video chat services will push revenues derived from mobile adult services to nearly $3.5 billion by 2010.

Holden, Windsor. <u>Mobile Adult: Subscriptions, Downloads, Video Chat & Text-Based Services 2007-2012</u>. 4th ed. Juniper Research, 2007.

News Stat

Vivid, a leading adult entertainment company based in Los Angeles, says that **50% of its mobile browser traffic now comes from iPhones.**

Caplan, Jeremy. "Turning the iPhone into the xxxPhone." <u>TIME</u> 18 June 2008. <http://www.time.com/time/business/article/0,8599,1815934,00.html>.

II Mainstreaming of Pornography via the Internet

A) Pornography is big business.

1) The pornography industry has grown to a $97 billion business worldwide; $13 billion of that business is here in the United States.

2) Internet pornography in the United States is a $3 billion industry.

Pornification of Youth

INTENTIONAL ACCESS

1 out of **3** youth who viewed pornography, viewed intentionally.

Source: Wolak, Janis, Kimberly Mitchell, and David Finkelhor. <u>Online Victimization of Youth: Five Years Later</u>. Alexandria, Virginia: National Center for Missing & Exploited Children, 2006.

ACCIDENTAL ACCESS

7 out of **10** youth have accidentally come across pornography.

Source: <u>Generation M: Media in the Lives of 8-18 Year-olds</u>. Henry J. Kaiser Family Foundation. 17 Nov. 2006.

B) Pornography has become the wallpaper of our children's lives.

1) It is intrusive, anonymous, private, and free.

2) Nearly 80% of the unwanted exposure to Internet pornography is taking place in the home.

Unwanted Exposure
Where the Material Was Seen

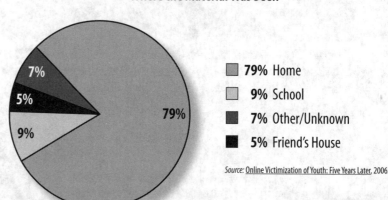

- **79%** Home
- **9%** School
- **7%** Other/Unknown
- **5%** Friend's House

Source: <u>Online Victimization of Youth: Five Years Later</u>, 2006.

C) Marketing Tactics of Pornographers

The pornography industry often uses many different marketing tactics to attract viewers and lure kids, and their marketing models create no incentive to distinguish between child and adult traffic. In fact, most pornography sites do not request age verification of their visitors and even offer free samples of pornographic images. Some of the "responsible" pornography sites include an entry page that warns viewers to only enter if they are over 18, but in reality, anyone can gain access by simply clicking on a link that reads, for example, "I am 18 years or older."

1) Free Teaser Images

Pictures and/or streaming videos to draw users in, including:

⊙ Nudity

⊙ Sexual activity of every form (i.e., sexual intercourse, masturbation, bisexual interactions, group sex, oral sex, fetishes)

⊙ Cybersex and cyberchats with "live" feeds (i.e., user can view and/or interact in real time with porn star)

⊙ Site "tours" (i.e., walks user through a virtual table of contents of pictures, videos, and pornographic experiences available)

2) Innocent Word Searches

Pornographic website operators use popular terms or innocent words that may have little or nothing to do with the content they display to increase traffic to pornographic sites. When a child keys in his or her favorite search term, pornographic sites pop up along with the sites the child is seeking.

ex.) _____

3) Misspelled Words

ex.) _____

■ **40% of youth** who came across pornography did so by conducting an innocent word search.[2]

4) Stealth Sites

Online pornographers often purchase "Stealth URLs." These are sites with web addresses that are close in name to the "legitimate" site. *(Example: Virginiapta.org once contained pornographic images. This site has been taken down since the making of the video.)*

■ *ADVICE: Organizations and high-profile individuals should purchase all domains which include their name as a preventative measure.*

"Pornography is not even considered a big deal in teenage society right now."

♀ Allie, Age 18

Through the Internet, pornography has become:

◐ Accessible to anyone;

◐ Anonymous; and

◐ Affordable (and often free).

INNOCENT WORD SEARCHES
ANSWER: water sports

MISSPELLED WORDS
ANSWERS: Faecbook vs. Facebook

[2] Wolak, Janis, Kimberly Mitchell, and David Finkelhor. Online Victimization of Youth: Five Years Later. Alexandria, Virginia: National Center for Missing & Exploited Children, 2006.

Unwanted Exposure to Sexual Material How Website Came Up

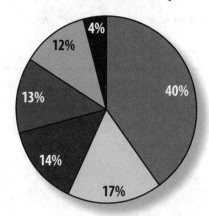

- **40%** Link came up as a result of search
- **17%** Clicked on link when in other site
- **14%** Pop-up
- **13%** Other
- **12%** Misspelled web address
- **4%** Don't know

2% of youth returned to the website

Source: <u>Online Victimization of Youth: Five Years Later</u>, 2006.

5) Cartoon Characters and Child Icons

6) Pop-ups & Ad Banners

Many popular sites and social networking spaces have advertising/ banner space for purchase. Pornographers often purchase this space hoping to draw young users to their sites.

7) Free Flash Games

A simple, interactive game, usually integrated into a website of similar games that can be played quickly, with little learning curve and no need to save the game's progress. Popular genres include puzzle games, word games, card games, and uncomplicated animated games.

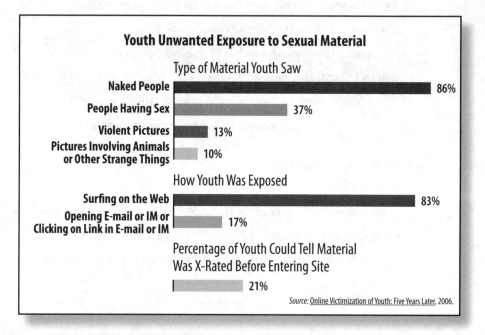

Youth Unwanted Exposure to Sexual Material

Type of Material Youth Saw
- Naked People — 86%
- People Having Sex — 37%
- Violent Pictures — 13%
- Pictures Involving Animals or Other Strange Things — 10%

How Youth Was Exposed
- Surfing on the Web — 83%
- Opening E-mail or IM or Clicking on Link in E-mail or IM — 17%

Percentage of Youth Could Tell Material Was X-Rated Before Entering Site — 21%

Source: <u>Online Victimization of Youth: Five Years Later</u>, 2006.

Did You Know...

Pornography is often interwoven into games and virtual reality sites?

- Many virtual reality communities now allow users to live out their sexual fantasies in the online world.

- Some sites include virtual red light districts, sex shops, swingers clubs, and opportunities to try out endless positions and combinations.

- Some mainstream online games also include explicit sexual interactions, even if the games are not obviously or explicitly sexual in nature.

> **ADDITIONAL MARKETING TACTICS NOT MENTIONED IN VIDEO INCLUDE:**
>
> - **E-mail Spam** ("junk e-mail")
>
> - **Mousetrapping:** This crafty tech-trick prevents user from escaping a pornographic site.
>
> - **Looping:** A seemingly never-ending stream of pornographic pop-ups to the computer screen. The only way to stop the pop-ups is to shut down the computer.
>
> - **Porn-Napping:** Pornographers purchase expired domain names so what was once a legitimate web address for a benign company or site now takes users to a pornographic site (see Stealth Sites).

III Isn't Pornography Just "Harmless Fun?"

A) The Effects of Pornography Can Be Life Altering

Pornography:

1) Has a negative impact on the emotional and mental health of children

2) Fosters sexual "mis-education"

3) Is a counterfeit for erotic love and intimacy

4) Diminishes sexual satisfaction

5) Teaches "Adult Entertainment" is normal and desirable

6) Desensitizes the viewer and increases an appetite for more deviant, bizarre, or violent types of pornography

7) Contains images that can never be erased

8) Facilitates sexual aggression

9) Can lead to objectification (obsessive fetishes over body parts and the rating of women by size and shape)

> *"There are a couple of images that stuck in my mind. I'd just be sitting there and all of a sudden, it'd pop up in my mind, and I'd be like 'whoa, why am I thinking about that?'"*
>
> ♀ Meghan, Age 15

Internet pornography is blamed for a **20% increase in sexual attacks** by children in the last three years.

"Web Is Blamed for 20 Percent Leap in Sex Attacks by Children." This is London. 3 Mar. 2007, <www.thisislondon.co.uk>.

Males aged between 12 and 17 who regularly viewed porn had sex at an earlier stage in their lives and were more likely to initiate oral sex, apparently imitating what they had watched. **Experts warned that the rise in the viewing of pornography was implicated in a variety of sexual problems**—including a rise in levels of STDs and teenage pregnancies—and called for parents to be more aware of what their children were watching. Women who had watched pornography at similar ages—a lower percentage than men—became sexually active slightly younger.

Hamill, Jasper. "Internet porn 'encourages teenagers to have sex early.'" Scotland's Sunday Herald. 26 Apr. 2008.

10) Can lead to "acting out"

11) Can lead to increased sexual callousness toward women

12) Can cause some to trivialize rape as a criminal offense

B) Pornography's Effects on Generation XXX

Attitudes in young men and women (18-26 years) after viewing pornography revealed:

1) An increase in the number of sexual partners

2) An increase in the acceptance of casual sex

3) An increase in the likelihood of substance abuse

4) A greater acceptance of extramarital affairs for men

For the first generation to grow up with Internet pornography, the impact is clear:

○ Roughly **two-thirds (67%)** of young men and **one-half (49%)** of young women agree that viewing pornography is acceptable.[3]

○ Nearly **9 out of 10 (87%)** young men and nearly **one-third (31%)** of young women report using pornography.[4]

Young men and women who use pornography:

○ Were more accepting of non-marital cohabitation; and

○ Displayed strong desires for later marriage and financial independence between spouses within marriage, and less desire for children.[5]

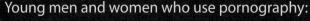

[3,4,5] Carroll, Jason S., et al. "Generation XXX: Pornography Acceptance and Use Among Emerging Adults." Journal of Adolescent Research 23.1 (2008) 6-30. (Study examined population of emerging adults aged 18-26.)

Ⅳ Empowering Parents

A) My child has stumbled upon online pornography—now what?

First, try to:

1) Understand that children are naturally curious about sex

2) Realize that kids need and want adult guidance

3) Educate your child about healthy sexuality, respect for themselves and the opposite sex

4) Help your child to replace counterfeit messages with messages of wholesome sexual values

B) Keep the lines of communication open by listening to what your kids say and don't say.

Ask your children:

1) Have you ever seen something online that made you uncomfortable or curious?

2) Have you accidentally seen sexual pictures online?

3) How did that happen? What did you do? How did it make you feel?

4) Have any of your friends ever accessed pornography? Accidentally or intentionally?

Ⓥ Warning Signs That a Child May Be Viewing Pornography

Experts in the field of childhood sexual abuse report that any premature sexual activity in children always suggests two possible stimulants: experience and exposure.

Your child may be viewing pornography if you discover the following:

⊙ An unusual curiosity about sexuality for his or her age

⊙ Signs of premature sexual activity

⊙ Unusual or unexplained credit card charges

⊙ Increased pop-ups or inappropriate e-mails on your computer

⊙ Computer screen changes quickly when you walk into a room

⊙ Noticeable changes in behavior, including increased secretiveness or defensiveness

Question:
Don't all pornographic sites require a credit card to gain access?

Answer:
No, teaser ads and pop-ups can lead anyone (including children!) to unlimited pornographic material—all for free!

THE PORNIFICATION OF OUR YOUTH

In the past, those who wanted to view hard-core pornography, particularly that which might be prosecutable, had to overcome the embarrassment of others watching them enter an adult bookstore or peep show. With the advent of the Internet, pornography has become mainstream, viewable by anyone, anywhere, anytime. Even when kids aren't looking for it, it finds them!

"I think about every person in this generation and probably the one before us have all looked up pornography once in their life. Even if you're not looking for it, you could be innocent on the computer...and it'll find you."

♂ Zach, Age 15

Viewing pornography has become the norm for many of today's youth

- It has become socially acceptable for boys and girls to use pornography

- Pornography is the "wallpaper" of our kids' lives

THE POWER OF PORNOGRAPHY: A CLOSER LOOK INTO THE DRUG CHOICE OF THE MILLENNIUM

Exposure to Pornography Shapes Attitudes and Values

As parents, most of us want to instill our own personal values about relationships, sex, intimacy, love, and marriage in our children. Unfortunately, powerful, misleading messages portrayed in Internet pornography may be taking the lead in educating children on these very important life issues. Just as 30-second commercials can influence whether we choose one popular soft drink over another, exposure to pornography shapes our attitudes and values and, often, our behavior.

Photographs, videos, magazines, virtual games, and Internet pornography that depict rape and the dehumanization of females in sexual scenes constitute powerful but deforming tools of sex education. Replicated studies have demonstrated that exposure to significant amounts of increasingly graphic forms of pornography has a dramatic effect on how adult consumers view women, sexual abuse, sexual relationships, and sex in general. ▪▪

"The images don't leave your mind, and I think that it plays a big part in how you see women you're attracted to. You don't just see them as, 'oh, she's pretty,' you see them as, 'wow—she's got a nice body'. And then you start picturing things that you saw." ♂ Kyle, Age 15

"It destroyed our lives, because we depended on it, and it just broke friendships, it broke relationships, it broke, like, respect for ourselves and our respect for others." ♀ Courtney, Age 18

Exposure to Pornography Has a Negative Impact on the Emotional and Mental Development of Children

As they grow up, children are especially susceptible to influences affecting their development. Information about sex in most homes and schools comes, presumably, in age-appropriate incremental stages based on what parents, educators, physicians, and social scientists have learned about child development. Research shows pornography short-circuits and distorts the normal personality development process and supplies misinformation about a child's sexuality, sense of self, and body that leaves the child confused, changed, and damaged. Pornography often introduces children prematurely to *sexual sensations that they are developmentally unprepared to contend with*. This awareness of sexual sensation can be confusing and overstimulating for children. ▪▪

Brain Imaging Studies

As we've heard in the video from Dr. W. Dean Belnap, a distinguished pediatrician and child and adolescent psychiatrist, during certain critical periods of childhood, a child's brain is being programmed for sexual orientation. It is during this period, he states, that the mind appears to be developing a "hardwire" for what the person will be aroused by or attracted to. Exposure to healthy sexual norms and attitudes during this critical period can result in the child developing a healthy sexual orientation. In contrast, if there is exposure to pornography during this period, thoughts of sexual deviance may become imprinted on the child's "hard drive" and become a permanent part of his or her sexual orientation.

Studies have shown that the prefrontal part of the brain that controls common sense, judgment, and emotion is not mature until approximately 21 years of age. These studies suggest that teens' brains are vulnerable and that teens, when exposed to Internet pornography or the barrage of sexually explicit content around us, may not be able to process this type of imagery in a healthy way. ▪▪

 "One of the cruelest and most distorting messages that the pornography industry gives people of all ages is that pornography will aid them in becoming sexually confident, sexually aware, and be better able to relate to a partner." ♀ Jill Manning, Ph.D., Marriage and Family Therapist

"The imprinting can become at times so strong that the individual can never gain satisfaction by giving; they always want to be taking. And it's never satisfying, as it was perhaps at one time along the way, because it requires more and more of the stimulus to keep up with their sexual desires."

♂ W. Dean Belnap, M.D. Pediatrician and Child and Adolescent Psychiatrist

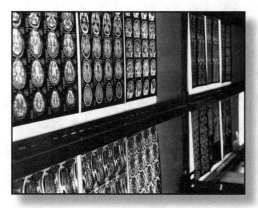

"I realized I was addicted when I tried to stop, and then I couldn't. I couldn't think of anyone without sex, and I always thought of the porn, and I kept thinking about it, until I had to give in. I had to watch porn so I could just go to sleep. If I didn't watch porn one night, I wouldn't go to sleep because I wanted it so much. So I'd watch porn every night, and it would make me go to sleep, I didn't even like it anymore." ♂ Augey, Age 17

Compulsive Habituation

In her report before Congress, Dr. Jill Manning, a marriage and family therapist who specializes in research and clinical work related to pornography and problematic sexual behavior, noted that studies show when a child or adolescent encounters Internet pornography, it can have lasting negative or even traumatic effects on the child's sense of security and sexuality; that it promotes the belief that superior sexual satisfaction is attainable without having affection for one's partner, thereby reinforcing the commoditization of sex and the objectification of humans; and that children

A CLOSER LOOK

Pornography's Progressive Pattern

STEP 1: Addiction
Once hooked, consumers come back for more and more

STEP 2: Escalation
Consumer requires more and more stimulation to reach "highs"

STEP 3: Desensitization
Material once perceived as unthinkable or shocking is now acceptable

STEP 4: Acting Out Sexually
A tendency to act out sexually the behaviors viewed in pornography

Adapted from Cline, Victor B. "Pornography's Effects on Adults and Children" 3-5.

"*Little girl's brains are being altered in the same way that the little boy brains are being altered...we're seeing increasing numbers of women engaging in sexual abuse and little girls sexually abusing other children as well, including their siblings. They're imitating what they see. Children are doing what children are supposed to do....Does it destroy them? Yes, it does. Is it their fault? No, it's our fault.*"

♀ Judith Reisman, Ph.D., President, The Institute for Media Education

who have been exposed have an increased risk for developing sexual compulsions and addictive behavior.

Once consumers of pornography are hooked, they keep coming back for more and more. The sexually graphic material provides the viewer with an aphrodisiac effect, followed by sexual release. Dr. Victor Cline, a clinical psychologist at the University of Utah and a specialist in the area of sexual addictions, has observed that the pornography consumer, similar to the drug user, requires more and more stimulation to reach the sought-after sexual "high." This escalation feeds complete desensitization, during which material that was originally perceived as unthinkable, shocking, illegal, repulsive, or immoral becomes commonplace. The last step that Dr. Cline observed is an increased tendency to act out sexually the behaviors viewed in pornography, and "acting out" is exactly what we are now seeing in today's youth. ▪

Exposure to Pornography May Incite Children to Act Out Sexually Against Other Children

There's no doubt that children often imitate what they've seen, read, or heard. When children watch cowboys and Indians, they want to go play cowboys and Indians. When children watch Superman, they pretend to be action heroes. When kids watch sex, it's no surprise they want to act out sexually. Some studies suggest that exposure to pornography can prompt kids to act out sexually against younger, smaller, and more vulnerable children.

As Internet pornography has continued to grow, clinicians, psychologists, and law enforcement officials have noted an increase in the number of children seeking clinical help for issues relating to sexual exploitation; an increase in the number of children "acting out" sexually and a jump in the incidences of child-on-child sex attacks; increased incidences of child-produced pornography; and trends in the worst forms of pornography. ▪

RULES OF ENGAGEMENT

With such a vast variety of information and images found online, the Internet has opened up a whole new set of topics for parents to discuss with their children. Most of us find it difficult to talk to our children about sex in general, let alone the harmful effects of pornography. Yet it's important to remember that even if your children are not looking for Internet pornography, chances are that they have come across this harmful content at some point, and it is your job to protect and guide them about their natural questions about sex.

As a parent or guardian, it is critical to keep the lines of communication open by talking to your children about inappropriate material. If your

children are exposed to pornography or if you find that they use pornography, don't overreact or shame them—children are naturally curious about sex.

Kids need and want adult guidance; educate your children about healthy sexuality and replace the counterfeit messages they receive from online pornography with wholesome messages of virtues and values. Teach them to respect themselves; teach them that they have worth and dignity, and educate them about the harms of pornography so they can make wise choices about what they view online. ⊞

"If I was a parent, I'd want to establish that relationship with my kid and to actually be honest with them and talk to them, and say ya'know, 'I went through this, and even seeing it once can just hurt you so much. Seeing little pictures can put all these things in your mind.' It's horrible."

♂ Aaron, Age 19

"...don't be judgmental. That's the worst thing a parent can do. Because it makes them feel they're not loved and that you know, 'why even bother stopping?' That's how I would feel."

♀ Kelly, Age 18

Rene's Story:

How Internet Pornography Invaded Her Home and the Hearts of Her Family

Rene is an attorney and part-time law professor who gave up active practice to be at home with her children. She and her husband devoted their lives to protecting their children and raising them in a safe and loving environment. Nine years ago, their lives and the life of their then 11-year-old son, Joe,* were forever changed when Joe became a victim of the lure of Internet pornography.

At the time, Rene and her husband kept their only computer in the "office" room of their home. As far as they were aware, they were the only ones who knew how to access the Internet. It never crossed their minds that their son knew how to gain access to the Internet, let alone locate pornographic material online.

> *"It's more addictive than crack cocaine and so invasive in the home."*
>
> ♀ Rene
> Mother of Internet Pornography Victim

So when her husband discovered a "minimized" pornographic site at the bottom of their computer screen, they were both in shock. But that shock was nothing compared to what they felt when a check of the Internet history revealed that their young, innocent son had visited more than 900 pornographic sites during the middle of the previous few nights. When lovingly confronted by his parents, Joe shared that he learned about a website containing pornographic images from a friend at school. Later, Rene and her husband discovered Joe's friend didn't even own a computer. From the start, Joe was deeply ashamed and felt the need to lie about his actions.

Joe's parents immediately placed passwords and filters on their computer, but the damage was already done. During the ensuing years, Joe tried to access pornography online to "feed" his addiction, while his parents tried everything they could think of to keep him from it. For example, while his friends were freely using the Internet to keep in touch with each other, Rene and her husband only allowed him to send e-mails while in their presence. Rene made it a common practice to send Joe out of the room before she would type in her password and then would close down the computer immediately after he sent his e-mails. However, as she later learned, even that was not enough to prevent Joe from viewing countless graphic images available online.

After one of these times of allowing him "restricted" access, Rene discovered that Joe had been up all night viewing pornography again. Upon questioning Joe, he revealed to Rene that he had placed a video camera on a bookshelf above the computer keyboard and filmed her fingers as she typed in her password. He shared how he had spent hours replaying the video until he was able to "decode" the finger strokes of her password using a paper keyboard he had made just for this purpose. As for the filters they had installed, Joe (as many kids do) figured out ways to get around them.

Rene and her husband were baffled by how such a young child could even get to pornography online, as he had no credit card. They learned that anyone can access very graphic pornographic images and video clips online at no cost. In fact, Joe never spent one dime on the pornography he viewed. The teaser ads and pop-ups were sufficient to take him to site after site linked one to another, thus providing an unlimited amount of free pornographic material.

Now, Joe was not a "bad kid," nor was he from a family that didn't care or that was uninvolved in his life. He was a bright, normally curious kid who—through exposure at a very impressionable age—succumbed to the addictive potential of Internet pornography. As often happens with any "addiction," the more Joe was exposed to pornographic images, the greater his desire for harder-core

material became. The graphic images "burned" into his brain have had lasting implications in his life related to relationships, frustration, shame, depression, lying, and anger.

Joe is now 20 years old and, even though he has had counseling, he is still dealing with the temptation to use this readily available type of pornography as an "escape," along with the resulting shame. Today, Rene continues to share her personal experiences to alert other parents to the detrimental effects of Internet pornography. She does so with the hope that they will avoid the trauma she and her family have known. As she warns, "This insidious thief of our children's innocence can walk right into our homes, uninvited and unannounced." She then adds, "Prevention is the best defense." ▪▪

Real names have been omitted

Discussion Questions

> How have the types of pornographic images changed over the past several decades?

> What effects have these graphic images had on children?

> What are some of the ways that teens encounter pornography online? Is it always their fault when they do view it?

> Why don't we have the same laws online that we have in print and other media? How does this place an increased unprecedented burden on parents to be the first line of defense to protect their children from cyberpornography?

> What should you do if you discover your child has viewed pornography (intentionally or unintentionally)?

How Cyber Savvy Are You?

1. On the Internet, pornography can be found:

a) In e-mail

b) On websites

c) In pop-ups and ad banners

d) All of the above

2. Which statement is true?

a) Soft-core and hard-core pornography can be found on the Internet.

b) Pornography is one of the most profitable businesses on the Internet.

c) Pornography can be defined as sexually explicit material intended primarily to arouse the reader, viewer, or listener.

d) All of the above

3. Which examples below would most likely be considered "Harmful to Minors" (pertaining to print) or "indecent" (pertaining to broadcast)?

a) Self breast exam diagram

b) *Sex In the City* TV show

c) Playboy channel

d) Victoria's Secret catalogue

e) Michelangelo's "David" in an art history book

f) *Penthouse* magazine

(Hint: If it's available for minor children in print or primetime broadcast, it's probably not legally considered indecent or harmful to minors.)

4. In which of the following circumstances should I consider seeking professional help for my child?

a) If or when my child accidentally comes across pornography

b) When my teenage daughter starts dressing provocatively

c) When I find that my child has been looking at pornography regularly and I find a lot of pornography on the computer

d) When I discover my child has been experimenting sexually with his baby sister

5. The best strategies for helping a child who has been traumatized by viewing pornography is:

a) Don't tell anyone about the incident.

b) Check out the child's story because children are prone to lie.

c) Try to alleviate any self-blame your child might be feeling for viewing pornography.

d) Talk to your child about healthy sexuality versus pornographic misinformation.

6. Which is NOT one of the deceptive tactics used by online pornographers to lure kids?

a) Mousetrapping

b) Pop-ups and ad banners

c) Stealth sites

d) Cruising

If you answered all questions correctly, congratulations! You are several steps closer to helping your children become safer online!

Answers: (1) D; (2) D; (3) C and F; (4) C and D; (5) C and D; (6) D

Important Sites to Know

● To report child pornography
   www.cybertipline.com

● To report obscenity
   www.obscenitycrimes.org

Question:
What can I do to encourage the enforcement of existing laws?

Answer:
Contact your elected officials including the State & U.S. Attorneys General, State U.S. Attorneys, and members of Congress (see Appendix D-2 for ways to contact elected officials).

She's somebody's daughter
Somebody's child
Somebody's pride and joy
Somebody loves her for who
she is inside
She has a mother and father
She's somebody's daughter

Lyrics taken from "SOMEBODY'S DAUGHTER," a song describing women depicted in pornography.
Words & Music by John Mandeville & Steve Siler

© 2005 Silerland Music (Administered by the Copyright Company) ASCAP / Lifestyle of Worship BMI

Empowering Parents

For a variety of resources on the harms of pornography, sexual addiction, and sexual abuse, visit:

Victims Assistance Resources at www.enough.org

Should I Seek Help for My Child?

If you should find that your child has been exposed to online pornography, it would be natural for you as a parent to wonder if you need to seek professional help for your child. Initially, it will be important to ascertain the severity of the pornographic content your child viewed. Were the images seen limited to images of body parts? Did they include graphic sexual acts, violence, or bestiality? Did the child later imitate aspects of what he or she saw on another sibling or child? (Many parents wisely seek the help of a therapist at this point to safeguard their role as a parent and avoid harming the parent-child relationship by making their child feel ashamed as they ask these difficult questions.)

Oftentimes, the decision to seek outside professional help is made on a case-by-case basis and depends on the child's age. For example, if your teenage child accidentally stumbled upon pornographic images and had an open discussion about what was seen with you, then chances are you may determine that you do not necessarily need to seek help for your child. However, if a child is clearly traumatized by the images viewed online, regularly views pornography, or later "acts out" against another child, you will want to consider seeking the help of a trained therapist.

The key is not to overreact or shame your child; rather, create an open and loving environment where you and your child can openly discuss what has been seen. Then, you will be able to better determine the appropriate course of action. Regardless of what was viewed, the goal is to help heal your child and relieve any suffering he or she may be experiencing—not to punish your child.

Enough Is Enough is pleased to offer a variety of secular and faith-based resources including suggested readings, audio and videotapes, CDs, and Internet resources to those searching for healing from the harms of pornography, sexual addiction, and sexual abuse. For more information, please visit our victim's resources at: **www.enough.org**.

An ounce of prevention is worth a pound of cure.

For more information about protecting your children on the Internet, visit the Safety 101 section.

Notes:

_____

_____

_____

_____

_____

_____

_____

_____

_____

_____

_____

_____

_____

_____

_____

_____

_____

_____

_____

_____

SEGMENT 2
PREDATORS 101

Introduction

When children go online, they have direct and immediate access to friends, family, and complete strangers, which can put unsuspecting children at great risk. Children who meet and communicate with strangers online are easy prey for Internet predators.

Predators have easy and anonymous access to children online where they can conceal their identity and roam without limit. Often, we have an image of sexual predators lurking around school playgrounds or hiding behind bushes scoping out their potential victims, but the reality is that today's sexual predators search for victims while hiding behind a computer screen, taking advantage of the anonymity the Internet offers. With the explosion of the Internet into a powerful, worldwide medium, the danger to children, whether they are from New York or New Zealand, has dramatically increased.

"People that do not believe that their children could ever become victimized are living in an unrealistic world. Regardless if your child makes 'A's' or not, that child has the potential to become victimized through online technologies, so I think it is very important for parents of all socio-economic status and with all different roles in society to take this problem very seriously."

♀ Melissa Morrow
Supervisory Special Agent
Child Exploitation Squad
FBI

SEGMENT 2 GOALS:

TO TEACH YOU ABOUT:

✔ The modus operandi of a predator;

✔ The online behaviors that may put your children at risk to predators; and

✔ How to protect your children from becoming sexually exploited by Internet predation.

> *"Predators are hiding behind the anonymity of the Internet to target kids, to entice kids online—to try to persuade them to meet them in the physical world."*
>
> ♂ Ernie Allen
> President & CEO
> National Center for Missing & Exploited Children

Child Sex Abuse: Putting the Problem in Context

Research indicates that **1** in **4** girls and **1** in **6** boys will be sexually victimized before adulthood[1]; sadly, **30-40%** of these victims are abused by a family member and **50%** are abused by someone outside the family whom they know and trust.[2] Although the majority of this child sex abuse does not occur online, in the Internet age, offline sex abuse is fueled by pedophiles' unprecedented access to child pornography and exacerbated as perpetrators post pictures online of their exploits.

[1] Centers for Disease Control and Prevention. Prevalence of Individual Adverse Childhood Experiences, 1995-1997. <http://www.cdc.gov/nccd-php/ace/prevalence.htm>.

[2] United States. Dept. of Justice. Natl Institute of Justice. Youth Victimization: Prevalence and Implications. Apr. 2003. <http://www.ncjrs.gov/pdffiles1/nij/194972.pdf>.

Predators Online

The anonymity of the Internet provides the perfect camouflage for a seasoned predator to operate. The predator's knowledge of certain teenage subjects is as accurate as his or her calculated ability to speak teens' online lingo. Pedophiles and sexual predators use the Internet, with no limits, to exchange names and addresses of other pedophiles and of potential child victims. Hidden behind screen names that are pseudonyms, they gather and swap child pornography online with amazing speed and in amounts beyond our wildest imagination.

Offline, pedophiles have typically operated in isolation. Never before have pedophiles had the opportunity to communicate so freely and directly with each other as they do online. Their communication on the Internet provides validation—or virtual validation—for their behavior. They share their conquests, real and imagined. They discuss ways to contact and lure children online and exchange tips on seduction techniques, as well as tips on the avoidance of law enforcement detection. They use the technology of the Internet to train and encourage each other to act out sexually with children.

The Internet has fueled the deviant sexual behavior of predators due to their easy access to both child pornography and to children. Both ignite the sexual appetite of pedophiles. À la carte child pornography depicting kids of all shapes, sizes, ethnicities, and ages (even toddlers and infants!), is only a mouse click away. A predator may also scroll through the cache of pictures and videos posted by unsuspecting children on YouTube, social networking sites, and blogs, among others. Is it any wonder that the once "closet" pedophiles are acting out their sexual fantasies on real-life victims?

Direct access to unsuspecting children via e-mail, instant messaging, social networking sites, and chat rooms simplifies the sexual predator's efforts to contact and groom children. Additionally, some teens are placing themselves at risk and willingly talk about sexual matters with online acquaintances.

> *"Where Kids Play, Predators Prey"*
>
> ♀ Donna Rice Hughes
> President, Enough Is Enough

What Fuels Online Predators?

A) Easy and anonymous _____ to children

B) Risky online behavior of youth

C) Virtual validation (predators validate and encourage each other's sexual desires for children, exchange child pornography, and trade secrets and tactics to avoid law enforcement)

D) Law enforcement challenges

E) Easy access to "à la carte" child _____

Question:

What is driving the problem of online predators?

Answer:

Unprecedented easy and anonymous access to kids, risky online behaviors of teens, virtual validation, child pornography, and law enforcement challenges!

WHAT FUELS ONLINE PREDATORS?
ANSWERS: A) access, E) pornography

Child Abuse Domains and URLs 2004-2006

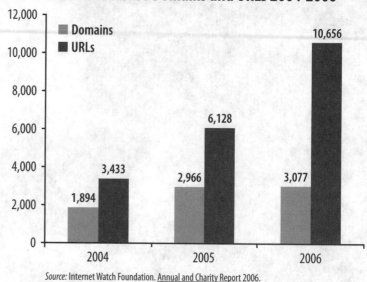

Source: Internet Watch Foundation. <u>Annual and Charity Report 2006</u>.

Child Sexual Abuse Levels

SENTENCING ADVISORY COUNCIL GUIDELINES	
Level	**Description**
1	Images depicting erotic posing with no sexual activity
2	Non-penetrative sexual activity between children or solo masturbation by a child
3	Non-penetrative sexual activity between adults and children
4	Penetrative sexual activity involving a child or children, or both children and adults
5	Sadism or penetration of or by an animal

47% of all child abuse websites depict the most severe
levels of child sexual abuse images (Levels 4 & 5).

Source: Internet Watch Foundation. <u>Annual and Charity Report 2006</u>.

Child pornography is one of the fastest growing industries on the Internet at $3 billion. As shown in the chart above, almost half of this child pornography is incredibly deviant, depicting sex acts between children, sex acts with adults, sadism, and bestiality.[3] Child pornography is addictive and the images can desensitize the viewer, generating a desire for more explicit and abusive images. Organizations fighting online child sexual abuse relay that the abuse is getting worse and the children depicted are getting younger— including infants. Every time a user clicks on one of these images of child sexual abuse, the child is re-victimized.

[3] Internet Watch Foundation. <u>Annual and Charity Report 2006</u>.
17 Apr. 2007. <http://www.iwf.org.uk/documents/20070412_iwf_
annual_report_2007_(web).pdf>.

Barely Legal!

The "adult entertainment" industry is promoting the sexual exploitation of children by displaying content they call "Barely Legal." Pornographers sell images depicting models and actresses who are legally adults, but look like they are significantly younger (i.e., 14 or 15 years old). These images further whet the appetites of men to desire younger and younger girls.

Ⅱ Online Sexual Solicitations: Fast Facts

A) One in _____ kids received a sexual solicitation online.[4]

B) _____% were asked to send a picture (27% of the pictures were sexually oriented!)

C) Not all convicted sex offenders have to _____ on the sex offender's registry.

D) Of the 614,006 convicted sex offenders in the United States, more than _____ registered convicted sex offenders have been "lost in the system."

Did You Know…

44% of the solicitors were under the age of 18!!![5]

Characteristics of Aggressive Sexual Solicitation of Youth Relationship to Solicitor

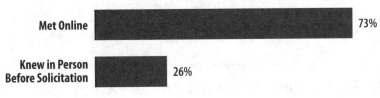

Met Online	73%
Knew in Person Before Solicitation	26%

Source: Online Victimization of Youth: Five Years Later, 2006.

ONLINE SEXUAL SOLICITATIONS: FAST FACTS
ANSWERS:
A) seven
B) 56
C) register
D) 102,000

[4] Wolak, Janis, Kimberly Mitchell, and David Finkelhor. Online Victimization of Youth: Five Years Later. Alexandria, Virginia: National Center for Missing & Exploited Children, 2006.
[5] Ibid

"Predators are in all professions. Unfortunately, we have seen doctors, lawyers, law enforcement, clergy, and members of the medical profession. There's really no common trait. In fact many of them are drawn to those particular professions which will give them access to children."

♀ Mary Beth Buchanan
U.S. District Attorney
Western Pennsylvania

Led the search for missing teen Alicia Kozakiewicz

III Profile of a Predator

What does an online predator "look like"?

Here's what the experts, as well as a convicted sex offender, told us. The online predator:

1) Blends into society

2) Is typically clean cut and outwardly law abiding

3) Is usually white, middle-aged or younger, and male

4) Uses position in society to throw off suspicion

5) Can rise to be a pillar of society while actively pursuing children

6) Often engages in activities involving children

7) Appears trusting to both parents and child

Bottom line: "You **CAN'T** detect a disguised online predator whether online or offline!"

♀ Donna Rice Hughes, President, Enough Is Enough

IV Grooming and Cyber Seduction

A) Predators "groom" children by:

1) Performing a _____ **assessment** to see if child is an easy target; they may introduce sexually explicit conversation immediately if a teen seems willing to engage with the predator.

- ⊙ "You sound cool."
- ⊙ "Do you need help with your homework?"
- ⊙ "What's your favorite band?"

2) Asking child if he or she wants to go **"private"** (by e-mail or through real-time, one-on-one communications such as instant messaging or other "chat" functions).

3) Predator begins **seduction.**

- ⊙ "How old are you?"
- ⊙ "What do you look like?"
- ⊙ "Do you have a picture?"
- ⊙ "Do you like older men?"

B) Where are these online encounters taking place?

Sexual solicitations of youth occur[6]:

1) Chatrooms (**37%**)

2) Instant messaging (**40%**)

3) Other—gaming devices (**21%**)

> "In the online world, predators use what we call 'grooming.' They build a relationship. They try to understand what they care about. They give them complements. Sometimes they'll even send presents or say nice things and eventually a teen will start having feelings for a predator and it's at that point where the danger begins."
>
> ♂ Hemanshu Nigam
> Chief Security Officer
> Fox Interactive Media
> and MySpace

> "One of the devices that predators use in the interactions with kids is sending them explicit photos of themselves. What they're trying to do is sort of deaden the nerve endings. They're trying to beat down the resistance. It's part of the grooming process to normalize what they're trying to do. And it's pretty insidious."
>
> ♂ Ernie Allen
> President & CEO, National Center for Missing & Exploited Children

GROOMING AND CYBER SEDUCTION
ANSWER:
1) risk

[6] Online Victimization of Youth: Five Years Later, 2006.

"In a period of a day in a three-hour period of time that I spent online I would probably talk to 25 children. When I would have initial contact with any individual, it would be my goal to find out what type of person it is that they were looking to speak to. So if it was a 13 or 14-year-old boy who was interested in speaking to a 13 or 14-year-old female, then I would be that female. There are millions of pictures online that you can download and send as far as this is who I am. And if it would get to a point where they would want to use the webcam or that type of thing, obviously I couldn't have anymore conversations...."

♂ "John Doe"
Convicted Sex Offender

Grooming Tactics of Predators

The following are additional ways predators groom their victims. While these are not mentioned at great length in the video, it is important for parents to be aware of the calculated methods used by online sexual offenders.

The predator often:

- Preys on teen's desire for romance, adventure, and sexual information

- Develops trust and secrecy: manipulates child by listening to and sympathizing with child's problems and insecurities

- Affirms feelings and choices of child

- Exploits natural sexual curiosities of child

- Eases inhibitions by gradually introducing sex into conversations or exposing them to pornography

- Flatters and compliments the child excessively, sends gifts, and invests time, money, and energy to groom child

- Develops an online relationship that is romantic, controlling, and upon which the child becomes dependent

- Drives a wedge between the child and his or her parents and friends

- Makes promises of an exciting, stress-free life, tailored to the youth's desire

- Makes threats, and often will use child pornography featuring their victims to blackmail them into silence

C) Acronyms to know

1) POS: _____

2) MIRL: _____

3) ASL(RP): _____

4) TDTM: _____

5) GNOC: _____

For a list of other acronyms, see Appendix A-31.

Ⓥ Risky Online Behaviors

A) The more risky behaviors kids engage in online,

the more likely they will receive an online sexual solicitation. These risky behaviors include:[7]

1) Posting personal _____ **(50%*)**

2) Interacting with online strangers **(45%)**

3) Placing strangers on buddy lists **(35%)**

4) Sending personal information to strangers **(26%)**

5) Visiting _____ sites **(13%)**

6) Talking about sex with strangers **(5%)**

* Percentage of teens demonstrating indicated risky behavior.

Like so many websites that can be misused, the popular YouTube site is no exception. A site search revealed thousands of graphic videos of young people in explicit scenes.[8]

"Most of the children that we see engaging in activities of a very sexually explicit nature on the Internet generally begin at about 12 and 14...where children are being enticed to engage in sexual activity online."

♀ Mary Beth Buchanan
U.S. District Attorney
Western Pennsylvania
Led the search for missing teen Alicia Kozakiewicz

ACRONYMS TO KNOW
ANSWERS:
1) POS: person over shoulder
2) MIRL: meet in real life
3) ASL(RP): age/sex/location (race, picture)
4) TDTM: talk dirty to me
5) GNOC: get naked on camera

RISKY ONLINE BEHAVIORS
ANSWERS:
1) information
5) X-rated

[7] Ybarra, Michele L., et al. "Internet Prevention Messages: Targeting the Right Online Behaviors." Archives of Pediatric and Adolescent Medicine, 161.2 (2007) 138-145 <http://archpedi.ama-assn.org/cgi/content/full/161/2/138>.

[8] Crawford, Carly and Geoff Wilkinson. "Teens main producers of child pornography." News.com.au 2 July 2008 <http://www.news.com.au/story/0,23599,23956258-421,00.html.com>.

Kid-Created Child Pornography: A Growing Trend

From music, to fashion, to celebrity culture, mainstream entertainment reflects an X-rated attitude like never before. Teens don "Porn Star" T-shirts and carry backpacks displaying the iconic Playboy symbol. Music videos are filled with stripper-inspired dancing and grinding, and college-aged girls flash cameras nonchalantly for inclusion in "Girls Gone Wild" videos.

Sexually explicit imagery can be seen in almost all advertising targeted toward teens and "tweens" in America—from toys, to clothing, music, movies, and video games. Today, some of the celebrities who capture teens' intrigue have created an infamous "sex tape" which only proves to *increase* their status. Is it any wonder that our sex-saturated culture has had a huge impact on our kids?

Teens, emulating their favorite celebrities, pose provocatively, take and send explicit pictures via digital cameras, cell phones and mobile devices (also called 'sexting'), and encourage one another to create and share videos of their sexual escapades. When minor children take and trade sexual images of themselves or their friends, they are in effect producing child pornography and can be prosecuted under the law. Never before have teens themselves generated so much child pornography!

"There's also a rise among teens of creating child pornography with their cell phones and camcorders...acts that they're doing with their boyfriends and girlfriends and then that is getting posted on the Internet and children are getting exploited sometimes by their peers."

♂ Jonathan Larcomb
Assistant Attorney General II
Computer Crimes Section, Office of the Attorney General
Richmond, Virginia

PREDOMINANT INTERNET SEX CRIME SCENARIO:
TWO SIDES OF THE STORY

A recent study found that many of the children who report becoming victims of Internet sex crimes describe themselves as "in love" with the sexual predators who offended against them. Police reports demonstrated that 80% of online offenders were eventually explicit about their intentions with youth, and only 5% of offenders concealed the fact that they were adults from their victims.[9] The teens met willingly, knowing they were interacting with an adult and would be engaging in sex. The victims were 13 to 15 years old, 75% girls and 25% boys; although girls were most often targeted, boys questioning their sexual orientation were also at greater risk. Pre-teens and teenagers (who are most vulnerable to online seduction) were most often their targets since they are more easily accessible in online chat rooms and through instant messaging—places where younger children aren't usually found.

In a separate study of 2,574 law enforcement agencies, researchers found that online sex crimes rarely involve offenders lying about their ages or sexual motives. The 2004 study, published in *Journal of Adolescent Health*, said offenders generally aren't strangers, and pedophiles aren't luring unsuspecting children by pretending to be a peer.[10] The study argued that the offenders could not be labeled as "strangers" because of the fact they had communicated with the victims over a long period of time, and victims felt close to the offenders before meeting.[11]

However, in Enough Is Enough's interviews with convicted sex offender "John Doe," and victim Alicia Kozakiewicz, deception was certainly employed. As John described:

> *"It would be my goal to find out what type of person it was that they were looking to speak to. So if it was a 13 or 14-year-old boy who was interested in speaking to a 13 or 14-year-old female, then I would be that female. There are millions of pictures online that you can download and send [to say] 'this is who I am.'"*

Researchers have noted a broad range in types of sexual offenders, from sadistic offenders who are focused on inflicting pain on a child and are most likely to abduct, harm, or murder a victim (i.e., Alicia's abductor) to those sexual offenders (referred to by some researchers as "seducers") who develop relationships over time, with any number of victims, for the purpose of forming a sexual relationship with a child, as was the case with John Doe.

[9] Wolak, Janis, Kimberly Mitchell, and David Finkelhor. "Internet-initiated sex crimes against minors: implications for prevention based on findings from a national study." <u>Journal of Adolescent Health</u>, 35.5 (2004) 424.e11-424.e20 <http://jahonline.org/article/PIIS1054139X04001715/fulltext>.

[10] Ibid.

[11] Ibid., 424.e18.

80% of online sex offenders were explicit about their intentions.[12]

John Doe indicated that at times he also was explicit about his intentions and desire for sexual interactions with the children with whom he communicated:

"I did not disguise what my true intentions were...the topic would come up...they would ask me if I had sex. They would ask me if I had a girlfriend or boyfriend depending on who they believed that they were talking to, talk about their sexual experiences... many times when I chatted online, it would be the children that I was talking to, especially the older children, 13 to 15, who would initiate the conversation that involved sex in some way or another."

In Alicia's case, she was introduced to her offender by a 42-year-old man pretending to be a red-haired, "teenage girl" named Christine, who had become a close and trusted online friend of hers.

What we must understand is that sexual predators may use a number of tactics to prey upon children: they may be explicit about their age and sexual interests to a willing teen; they may gradually reveal information during the grooming process; or, they may use deception to lure a child into a sexual relationship. Adults have a different knowledge and power base than children, and Internet predators are very adept at seducing and grooming children. The law clearly states that minors are incapable of consenting to sexual contact. Therefore, no matter how complacent or compliant the minor appears regarding the sexual contact, consent of the minor is no defense for sexual contact with the adult. It is always illegal to have sexual contact with a minor.

Another key point is that sexual predators are not always adults and not always strangers. Surveys show that teens are engaging in online sexual predation of other teens (i.e., peer-to-peer predation). Young people are at far higher risk of sexual predation from people in their family and community, all of whom may use the Internet to fuel their sexual appetite for children. ▪▪

[12] Wolak, Janis, Kimberly Mitchell, and David Finkelhor. National Juvenile Online Victimization Study (N-JOV) (2003). Crimes Against Children Research Center <http://www.unh.edu/ccrc/pdf/jvq/CV72.pdf>.

Alicia's Story

"I feel that I was rescued for a reason, and that reason is to save kids from the same thing happening to them... to show them that it can happen to them. This is real. This isn't a horror story or a movie; these people exist."

♀ Alicia Kozakiewicz

"Just because a child left without a struggle, doesn't mean they left willingly."

♀ Mary Kozakiewicz, Alicia's Mom

On New Year's Day 2002, 13-year-old Alicia Kozakiewicz disappeared from her suburban Pennsylvania home following a family dinner. Suspicions that Alicia may have been lured by someone she had met while chatting on the Internet proved to be true. For four days, Alicia was beaten, tortured, and raped while she was held captive in the basement by a 38-year-old computer programmer whom she met in an online chat room months earlier. The horrific images of Alicia's abuse were posted on the Internet by her abductor. Acting on a tip from one of her abductor's online acquaintances, authorities were able to track her to a townhouse in Virginia where they found her chained to the floor with a locked collar around her neck in what Alicia describes as a "dungeon."

Alicia originally developed a close online relationship with "Christine," whom she believed was a 14-year-old girl with long, red hair. Alicia later learned that "Christine" was a 42-year-old man, but in the online world where "identity" is often ambiguous, Alicia remained friends with "Christine." Eventually, "Christine" introduced Alicia to the man who would become her abductor.

Alicia's abductor is presently serving out a 20-year prison sentence. Alicia considers herself "one of the lucky ones," and she dedicated the National Center for Missing & Exploited Children's 2007 Courage Award to the many children who were killed or are still missing.

Alicia is determined to prevent other children from suffering her fate. Today she devotes her time speaking to students about the dangers they can face while online and warning them to avoid engaging in risky online behaviors. She is also the inspiration behind a proposal called Alicia's Law *(passed into law in Virginia in 2008)*, which provides state funding to law enforcement agents who target online criminals involved in child pornography and who attempt to lure children into face-to-face meetings.

While warning the U.S. Congress House Judiciary Committee against the dangers of Internet sex crimes in 2007, Alicia shared the harsh reality of the struggles she still faces today as a result of her horrific kidnapping. ***"I cry inside. I mourn for that child that was me. The child that was stolen from me. Make no mistake—that child was murdered. The boogey man is real. And he lives on the Net. He lived in my computer—and he lives in yours…While you are sitting here, he is at home with your children."*** ⠿

VI Warning Signs

Your child may be in contact with an online predator if he or she:

A) Becomes secretive about online activities

B) Becomes obsessive about being online

C) Gets angry when he or she can't get online

D) Receives phone calls from people you do not know or makes calls to numbers that you do not recognize

E) Receives gifts, mail, or packages from someone you do not know

F) Withdraws from family and friends

G) Changes screens or turns off the computer when an adult enters a room

H) Begins downloading pornography online

VII Important Resources

A) CyberTipline

The congressionally mandated CyberTipline is a reporting mechanism for cases of child sexual exploitation including child pornography, online enticement of children for sex acts, molestation of children outside the family, sex tourism of children, child victims of prostitution, and unsolicited obscene material sent to a child. Reports may be made 24 hours per day, 7 days per week online at **www.cybertipline.com** or by calling **1-800-843-5678**.

B) AMBER™ Alert

The AMBER Alert program is a voluntary partnership between law enforcement agencies, broadcasters, transportation agencies, and the wireless industry to activate an urgent bulletin in the most serious child-abduction cases. The goal of an AMBER Alert is to instantly galvanize the entire community to assist in the search for and the safe recovery of the child. (**www.amberalert.gov**)

C) Family Watchdog®

Family Watchdog enables site visitors to use its free service to locate registered sex offenders in their area. Simply enter an address and it will provide a map of any sex offenders within the vicinity. Enough Is Enough recommends that parents check the sex offender registry in their neighborhood, near their child's school, as well as other areas frequented by the child. (**www.familywatchdog.us**)

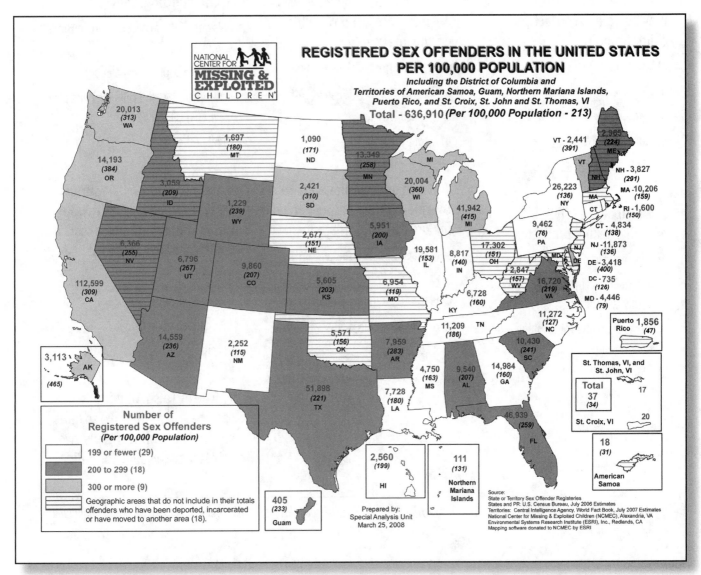

Discussion Questions

> What tactics did Alicia's predator use to groom her?

> How can parents talk to their children about online predators?

> What are some of the warning signs parents should recognize regarding their child's online behaviors?

How Cyber Savvy Are You?

1. While online, pedophiles may be able to contact your child through:

a) Instant messages (IMs)

b) Chat rooms

c) Unsolicited e-mail messages

d) Gaming devices

e) All of the above

2. Which of the following is true of online sexual predators?

a) They blend into society.

b) They are typically clean cut and outwardly law abiding.

c) They are usually white, middle-aged or younger, and male.

d) All of the above

3. Which of the following ways do predators "groom" children on the Internet?

a) They perform a "risk assessment."

b) They ask the child to "go private."

c) They seduce them.

d) All of the above

4. Which of the following are considered risky online behaviors for kids?

a) Interacting with strangers and sharing personal information

b) Placing a stranger on a buddy list

c) Visiting X-rated websites

d) All of the above

5. Child pornography:

a) Is one of the fastest growing businesses online

b) Fuels the appetite of a pedophile

c) Re-victimizes the child over and over when it is in circulation

d) All of the above

6. Recent studies have surprisingly revealed that a growing number of online sexual solicitations are being made by:

a) White middle-aged men

b) Juveniles under the age of 18

c) Convicted sex offenders

d) Females

7. True or False: Of youth who received an aggressive sexual solicitation online, nearly two-thirds met the solicitor online.

If you answered all questions correctly, congratulations! You are several steps closer to helping your children become safer online!

Answers: (1) E; (2) D; (3) D; (4) D; (5) D; (6) B; (7) True

> ## "Everyone Wants to Feel Loved"
>
> *"Grooming is really easy to understand once you give thought to it. Everybody wants to feel loved...and these people online are willing to make you feel that way. It never occurs to you that the person that you're talking to may be a monster. And they do it in the most subtle ways. You get in a fight with a friend. 'Your friend called you that? Oh my gosh. Why would your friend ever call you that? That's not a friend. I'm your real friend. I would never say anything like that.' And they pull you away from everything around you, all your friends and your family and your teachers. And as they're getting pulled away, you're getting closer to him. It's very similar to isolating somebody in an abusive relationship."*
>
> ♀ Alicia, teenage victim of online predator and NCMEC Courage Award Recipient (2007)

A Closer Look:
The Grooming Process

Children put themselves at great risk by communicating online with individuals they do not know in person. Internet predators intentionally access sites that children visit and can even search for potential victims by location or interest. If a predator is already communicating with a child, he or she can piece together clues from what the child mentions while online, including parents' names, where the child goes to school, and how far away the child lives from a certain landmark, store, or other location.

Online grooming is a process which can take place in a short time or over an extended period of time. Initial conversations online can appear innocent, but often involve some level of deception. As the predator (usually an adult) attempts to establish a relationship to gain a child's trust, he may initially lie about his age or may never reveal his real age to the child, even after forming an established online relationship. Often, the groomer will know popular music artists, clothing trends, sports team information, or another activity or hobby the

child may be interested in, and will try to relate to the child. These tactics lead children to believe that no one else can understand them or their situation like the groomer.

After the child's trust develops, the groomer may use sexually explicit conversations to test boundaries and exploit a child's natural curiosity about sex. Predators often use pornography and child pornography to lower a child's inhibitions and use their adult status to influence and control a child's behavior. They also flatter and compliment the child excessively and manipulate a child's trust by relating to emotions and insecurities and affirming the child's feelings and choices. **REMEMBER: The ultimate goal of the "groomer" is to arrange an in-person meeting to engage in sexual relations with the child or teen! ▦**

> *"I did whatever I had to do to survive..."*
>
> *"When kids ask why...I don't know why. I won't ever know why I went out that door because there is no logical reason that I would of. I hate the cold and am terrified of the dark. And it was the scariest, iciest night of the year. But, I went outside with no coat, no money. I didn't even go outside if my book bag was left in the car. I remember opening the door and feeling the wind bite my face and being at the top of the hill and hiding behind a tree. And when I said, 'You know what, why am I here?', for a moment, my senses came back...and, when I went to turn around, and he called my name, the very next thing I knew, I was in the car, and he was squeezing my hand so tight that I thought it was broken. And he said, 'Be good. Be quiet. I've got the trunk cleaned out for you.' At which point, I did whatever I had to do to survive. At which point, there was no fighting or screaming."*
>
> ♀ Alicia, teenage victim of online predator
> and NCMEC Courage Award Recipient (2007)

The M.O. of an Online Predator

It is the sexual preference and deviant desire of a pedophile to have illicit relations with a child. The sexual compulsion of an online predator is so strong, the pedophile will go to almost any length including extravagant plans that involve time, travel, and expense to arrange and meet with a child.

Predators will try to lure children into a face-to-face meeting by:

⊙ Developing an online relationship that is romantic, controlling, and upon which the child becomes dependent

⊙ Driving a wedge between child and parents and friends

⊙ Making promises of an exciting, stress-free life, tailored for what the youth wants

⊙ Making threats, and often using child pornography of their victim to blackmail them into silence

To learn more about the M.O. of an online predator, read excerpts from Enough Is Enough's interview with convicted sex offender "John Doe" in Appendix A-39. ▓

A Closer Look:
Who's At Risk?

With the advent of social networking sites and detailed chat profiles, predators don't need to work very hard to piece together information about a child online. Predators can judge by the appearance of a profile or by the behavior that a child is exhibiting whether he or she might be a prime target for an online relationship.

Teens who don't use privacy settings on social networking and gaming sites often place their information—including their deepest desires, likes and dislikes, real-time moods, pictures, addresses, and phone numbers—for anyone to see. Teens who post personal information, blog, or journal about sensitive issues may also be easy targets for predators who seek to isolate children from their parents and friends and exploit a child's emotional vulnerabilities.

Some teens think it's fun to flirt with online strangers, seek "hookups" with other teens and adults, and discuss and share images of their sexual exploits publicly. Those who use sexually inviting usernames, discuss sex online, and arrange to meet for sex place themselves at great risk. Also in danger of becoming targets are teens who are exploring sexual issues online—including sexual orientation—and those interested in meeting strangers online.

Teens who don't tell their parents when they meet someone or see something that makes them uncomfortable online are also at risk. Some experts suggest that these are vulnerable and at-risk teens to begin with, and are most likely to come from families where the parents are not sufficiently involved with their children. ▪

RULES OF ENGAGEMENT

Communication is key in protecting children from online exploitation. One way to keep children safer is to supervise their online activities or limit their access to sites that can facilitate online interaction with people they don't know and trust in real life. If you allow your children access to these sites, you should discuss Internet safety often. Monitor children's Internet use: ask them what sites they visit and to show you any profiles they may have posted online.

Parents need to:

- Pay attention to what your kids are doing online, and ask your child non-threatening questions.

- Avoid over-reacting if your kids have been talking to people they don't know online or if they admit that they've come across a dangerous or tricky situation online.

Ask: "Has an online stranger…

- Tried to befriend you? If so, how do you know this person?"

- Talked to you about sex?"

- Asked you for personal information?"

- Asked you for pictures? Sent you pictures?"

- Said anything to make you feel uncomfortable?"

- Offered to send you gifts?" ⊞

Advice from Mary and Alicia Kozakiewicz

Mary and Alicia serve on Enough Is Enough's Internet Safety Council.

MARY'S ADVICE: "When you speak to [your child], let them understand that you know children are online...engaging in various activities that, while you may not approve of them, you know have become very common, and that you're not going to go ballistic if they tell you that they're doing the same thing. You just want to discuss it and you want to keep them safe; it's not that you want to police them."

"Remember that it's okay to initiate a conversation. We're not invading their privacy, we're parenting. We seem to have forgotten that. We are the parents; we're not the friends. As children know more than we do, usually about technology, they've taken control, and, as a result, they're totally out of control."

"We don't feel it's amiss to smell their breath to see if they've been drinking, or to put limits on what they can do with the car. [We tell them] not to smoke [or] do drugs; there is absolutely no reason we cannot watch them and guard them by checking out what they're doing on the Internet, and they need to know we have the right to do that and agree with that right, just as they do in other areas."

ALICIA'S ADVICE: "Parents need to pay attention to their kids' [online] activities; they've got to stop just trying to be the child's friend and giving them all the privacy in the world...it's important to have blocks on the family's computer...to put monitoring software on the computer when your child is really young, so they grow with it [and] know it's there. But also have one that they don't know about, software that monitors all their activities, every key stroke...don't look at it every day, but if your child disappears, you have a road map, possibly, to their location...who wouldn't want that chance?"

"Online, it's really, really hard to define a stranger, because a lot of time, you'll talk to your real friend online from school, and then they introduce you to their friend from another school. Then that person will introduce you to their friend and to their friend, and then you are in a room of people that you don't know, but you all feel connected because you have that common string, that common friend... so don't just give your child that advice, 'don't talk to strangers.'"

"Your kids are curious about sex...they are...and they're looking for answers. Somebody online will answer them...somebody online would like to show them, and that's a really scary fact."

| A CLOSER LOOK |

***An ounce of prevention is worth
a pound of cure.***

To learn how to protect your children
from Internet predators, visit the
Safety 101 section.

Notes:

_____

_____

_____

_____

_____

_____

_____

_____

_____

_____

_____

_____

_____

_____

_____

_____

_____

_____

SEGMENT 3 THE EVOLVING INTERNET: WEB 2.0

Introduction

Our children are navigating an online world that can seem foreign and overwhelming to us as parents, but for our children, navigating this ever-evolving Internet, often referred to as Web 2.0, seems as natural as breathing. The evolving web is as much about what people upload as what they download. Cheaper, more accessible technologies now allow anyone to create a website, upload a video, or design and develop personal online spaces. The Web 2.0 world is mobile, multidirectional, and multi-media in format, allowing people to communicate through whichever medium they prefer.

"We adults are digital immigrants and they [children] are the digital natives and there are still a few adults who are in the old country. The Web 2.0 is highly collaborative, highly interactive, and our biggest challenge is how we help kids engage in this collaboration and interactivity in a safe and responsible manner."

♀ Nancy Willard, Director
Center for Safe and
Responsible Internet Use

SEGMENT 3 GOALS:

TO TEACH YOU ABOUT:
- ✔ How kids are using Web 2.0;
- ✔ Social networking benefits, dangers, and tips;
- ✔ Online gaming, its dangers, and tips to help protect your children; and,
- ✔ Cyberbullying, warning signs, and preventative measures.

The Evolving Internet

A) Web 1.0 vs. Web 2.0

The World Wide Web has transformed from a collection of websites to a full-fledged communicative platform, changing *where* and *how* we interact, share, and seek information. "Web 2.0" represents a paradigm shift in the way the Internet is used, facilitating creativity, information sharing, online communities, and collaboration among users.

WEB 1.0: "THE FIRST GENERATION OF THE WEB"	WEB 2.0: "THE NEW GENERATION OF THE WEB"
Users mainly downloaded information	Users can download and upload anything: text, music, pictures, and videos
Users had to wait for dial-up and had "desktop-only Internet access"	Users have instant, "anywhere access" using a variety of Internet-enabled devices

B) "Anywhere access": the mobile Internet

All of the powerful Internet resources available are now accessible through devices that fit in the palm of our hand. The "mobile Internet" allows instant communication to an unlimited number of individuals; children can upload content, videos, and photos through their cell phones and other portable devices, challenging the ability of parents to monitor their access online.

Internet-enabled devices:

1) Laptop computers

2) Cell phones (with camera, video, and Internet options)

3) Portable media players (MP3 players)

4) PDAs (personal digital assistants)

5) Gaming consoles

Sexting: A Growing Trend

What it is: Cell phone and other mobile, Internet-connected device users—often teens and 'tweens'—create and exchange provocative messages and nude, sexual images of themselves using their cell phone's built-in digital camera and text capabilities.

In a recent survey from the National Campaign to Prevent Teen and Unplanned Pregnancy, one out of five teens reported that they have 'electronically sent or posted online, nude or semi-nude pictures of videos of themselves.' With an estimated 90 to 95 percent of school kids carrying cell phones, this is a trend we cannot afford to ignore!

Be sure to disable, monitor or limit your child's picture text and chat options options, and remember to apply *Rules 'N Tools*® on your child's mobile device!

Youth Online Identity

Kids have historically used the Internet for many social purposes such as e-mailing and instant messaging. More recently, their means of interacting online have evolved to include activities such as creating and posting profiles and YouTube videos, blogging, and mobile texting.

The Internet allows kids to stay in touch and up to date with old friends and maintain large circles of friends from wherever they are. Researchers and psychologists say teens are using the web as a relatively safe place to try on different personas, interact, and figure out who they are in an important process of self-actualization. Teens are developing a fluency in expressing themselves through multiple types of digital media—most notably through the use of social networking sites.

Ⅱ Social Networking Sites

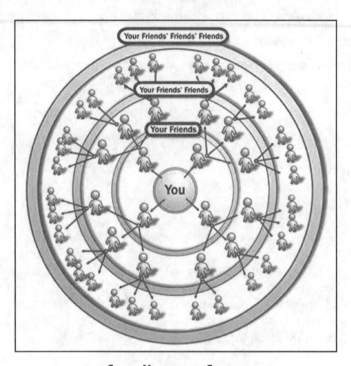

SOCIAL NETWORKING SITES =
PROFILES + BLOGS + ADS + PICTURES + VIDEOS + MUSIC + E-MAIL + IM + CHAT ROOMS

In the online world, social networking sites have become a predominant forum for kids to present themselves, seek approval, and describe their interests. One of the defining features of most social networking pages is the visual and audio clutter; these sites often look like over-decorated high school yearbooks or scrapbooks. Teens use these pages as a place to feature everything in their heads and hearts that they want people to know about. The central feature of these sites is the ability to connect with people and share information.

A) What is a social networking site?

1) Social networking sites are virtual communities.

2) Kids convene on these sites to chat, IM, post pictures, and blog (journal).

3) They appeal to teens because they provide instant community, instant celebrity, and encompass so many of the online tools and entertainment activities that teens know and love.[1]

4) They provide access to real-time and asynchronous communication features; blogging tools; photo-, music-, and video-sharing features (from the site itself and through a kid's cell phone and mobile device); and the ability to post original creative work—all linked to a unique profile that can be customized and updated on a regular basis.[2]

[1] Rosen, Christine. "Virtual Friendship and the New Narcissism." The New Atlantis, Summer 2007 <http://www.thenewatlantis.com/publications/virtual-friendship-and-the-new-narcissism>.

[2] Ibid.

B) What is an online "profile"?

1) Social networking sites allow users to create a "profile" space, which is essentially a user's online identity.

2) Often, the first components teens include in an online profile are[3]:

- ⊙ Real Age **(69%*)**
- ⊙ Photos or videos of themselves **(64%)**
- ⊙ City they live in **(58%)**
- ⊙ School name/location **(49%)**

* Percentage of teens demonstrating indicated behavior

Example of a social networking site profile

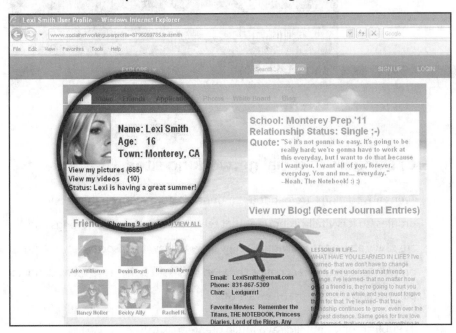

Additional information frequently posted by teens:

- ⊙ Full name
- ⊙ Birthday
- ⊙ Information about and photos of their friends
- ⊙ Dating status
- ⊙ "Life status"—including: how they are getting along with parents, with friends, at school, etc.

"Online"
Lyrics by country recording artist Brad Paisley

I work down at the Pizza Pit
And I drive an old Hyundai
I still live with my mom and dad
I'm 5 foot 3 and overweight
I'm a sci-fi fanatic
A mild asthmatic
And I've never been to second base
But there's whole 'nother me
That you need to see
Go checkout MySpace

'Cause online I'm out in Hollywood
I'm 6 foot 5 and I look damn good
I drive a Maserati
I'm a black-belt in karate
And I love a good glass of wine
It turns girls on that I'm mysterious
I tell them I don't want nothing serious
'Cause even on a slow day
I could have a three way
Chat with two women at one time
I'm so much cooler online
So much cooler online

Lyrics excerpted from Paisley, Brad. "Online."
5th Gear. Arista Nashville, 2007.

[3] Cox Communications Teen Internet Safety Survey, Wave II—in Partnership with the National Center for Missing & Exploited Children. March 2007 <http://www.cox.com/TakeCharge/includes/docs/survey_results_2007.ppt#271,1,Slide 1>.

An example of "Superpoking" online

```
▼ SuperPoke!                                    add
Your Friends | Mass Poke!                     See All
```

July 05

⏸ Suzette has ridden the Tour de France with Kate
July 5 11:41pm

March 19

Suzette has watched March Madness with Kate

February 20

Arda has thrown a fish at Kate

February 11

Marybeth has trout slapped Kate

Marybeth has wished 'Happy Birthday' to Kate

February 07

Suzette has wished a lucky year to Kate

February 05

Suzette has endorsed Kate

February 01

Suzette has celebrated Fat Tuesday with Kate

What do you want to do to Kate (just click & wait)   Options
bite, chest bump, dropkick, headbutt, high five, hug, kiss, lick, pet,
pinch, pwn, slap, spank, sucker punch, tickle, trip, worship, throw a
sheep at, more...

Online "E-props"

Kids can do many of the same things in the online world that they can do in the offline world including:

- High-fiving
- Poking
- Kissing
- Slapping
- Punching
- Humping

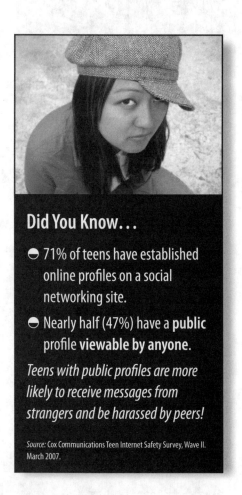

Did You Know…

- 71% of teens have established online profiles on a social networking site.
- Nearly half (47%) have a **public** profile **viewable by anyone**.

Teens with public profiles are more likely to receive messages from strangers and be harassed by peers!

Source: Cox Communications Teen Internet Safety Survey, Wave II. March 2007.

C) Dangers of social networking sites

Teens are posting a tremendous amount of information on their online profiles, so it is vitally important that teens use strict privacy settings and are savvy about the individuals they allow to view their social networking profile. As teens interact online through these sites, there are many dangers parents and teens must be aware of:

1) Public profiles put kids at a much greater risk to[4]:

   A) Receive a message from a stranger

   B) Meet with a stranger

   C) Be harassed by peers

2) Other concerns of social networking sites:

   A) Lack of _____-verification mechanisms

   B) Posting _____ pictures and videos

   C) Easy access for predators and _____

[4] Cox Communications Teen Internet Safety Survey, Wave II. March 2007.

D) Excessive or addictive access

E) Access to unhealthy "groups"

Examples: _____ _____

D) Social networking tips

Teach your child to:

1) Be as _____ as possible

2) Use privacy settings

3) Think before they post

4) Avoid in-person meetings

5) Be honest about their age

6) Remember social networking sites are public spaces

7) Avoid posting anything that could embarrass them later or expose them to danger

> *"Kids are going to post photos and personal information. At least they should be aware of the risks. At least they should use the privacy tools built into the sites to keep people they don't know from accessing their information and their data. And at least moms and dads should learn about what they are doing."*
>
> ♂ Ernie Allen, President & CEO National Center for Missing & Exploited Children

OTHER CONCERNS OF SOCIAL NETWORKING SITES
ANSWERS:
A) age
B) provocative
C) cyberbullies
E) cutting group, pro-marijuana, anorexia sites

SOCIAL NETWORKING TIPS
ANSWERS:
1) anonymous

Age Verification

With the popularity of social networking among youth, one of the issues of great concern is how to keep under-age users off of these sites. Although most sites require users to be at least 13 years of age, many children lie about their age in order to join these sites, risking exposure to content and activities suitable only for more mature teens.

In the offline world, clear mechanisms are in place to verify age, but the anonymous nature of the web makes it difficult to differentiate between an 11-year-old girl and a 60-year-old man. Although proactive social networking sites are utilizing mechanisms to kick off underage users and sex offenders alike, they maintain that age verification software is not effective for identifying and protecting minors who try to use their sites.

In 2008, at the urging of the Attorneys General of the United States, an Internet Safety Technical Task Force of industry and non-profit leaders, including EIE President Donna Rice Hughes, was established to explore how best to protect kids in the evolving social web. Stay tuned for more on this hotly debated issue.

* For a list of social networking sites appropriate for younger children please see Appendix B-12.

Do you Tweet?

Twitter is a social media site that lets its users send short messages (or "tweets") to a network of connected users online. Twitter is similar in form to features on other social networking and instant messaging sites that allow users to update their "status" or leave an "away message" to let their friends know what they are up to in real-time, all the time. On Twitter, this is also called "micro-blogging"; individuals have 140 characters to let the world know what's on their mind or to send a tweet about something they care about. Remember to use social networking safety tips on all social networking sites, whether it's Twitter or any other emerging site!

8) Remember that people aren't always who they say they are

9) Check comments regularly

10) Avoid inappropriate content and behavior, and, if encountered, report it to the social networking site

 Parents should search social networking sites their teens visit to see what information they are posting. Make sure you are added to your teen's "friend list" so you can view their information and verify that their profiles are set to private (as they should be!). If you're uncertain whether your child has a profile, do a simple online search by typing your child's name into a search engine like Google, or into the search option of the site in question.

Parents should be aware that YouTube users can communicate through and post information to the site, in ways similar to other social networking sites. EIE strongly recommends that if parents allow their children to use YouTube, that they establish a family account so parents can monitor the content posted and messages received through the site.

How to Report Abuse on a Social Networking Site

Learn what constitutes abuse according to the Social Networking Site's Terms and Conditions page. Click the 'Report Abuse' link and type a description of the abuse in the text field labeled 'Message.' Be sure to include a detailed description of the nature of the abuse you are reporting. Also, try to include the name or profile name of the person whom you are reporting, and submit it to the Social Networking Site.

If you feel you and/or someone you know are in danger, contact law enforcement immediately.

- Do not respond to messages from the individual and be sure to keep copies of messages or correspondences from the individual.
- Block the individual from contacting you and remove the individual from your "Friend List."
- Delete any comments the individual has left on your profile page.

SOCIAL NETWORKING SITES—A CLOSER LOOK
Friendship in the Web 2.0 World

We all love customized and personalized things, right? From monograms to picking out features in our automobiles, we all long for things that fit us "perfectly." We also all have a natural desire to be accepted and affirmed, and to put our "best foot forward."

One of the major reasons why teens are such enthusiastic users of social network sites is that the sites give them the opportunity to present fully customized, personalized representations of themselves to a group of peers—all the while anticipating feedback and affirmation from those who visit their site. Teens get to feel like they are a part of a group of like-minded friends and can visualize their network of relationships, displaying their popularity for others.

But "friendship" in these virtual spaces is thoroughly different from real-world friendship, traditionally based on shared experiences, trust, and revelation of information over time. Online, a user "friends" people—that is, invites them by e-mail or "message" to appear on the user's "Friend Space," where they are listed, linked, and ranked.

However, the Internet link called "friendship" on social networking sites is public, allowing "friends" to have access to all of the information included on your teen's social networking profile.

Some teens feel compelled to display big friendship networks to appear more "popular" online, and may be online "friends" with other social networkers whom they have never met in person. ▪▪

> "I used to have 400 friends, and some of them were just people I'd met online or added me, and I deleted all of them [except for] 60, because the 60 people were the only ones I was actually really friends with."
>
> ♀ Caroline, Age 16

A CLOSER LOOK

An example of being "friended" on a social networking site

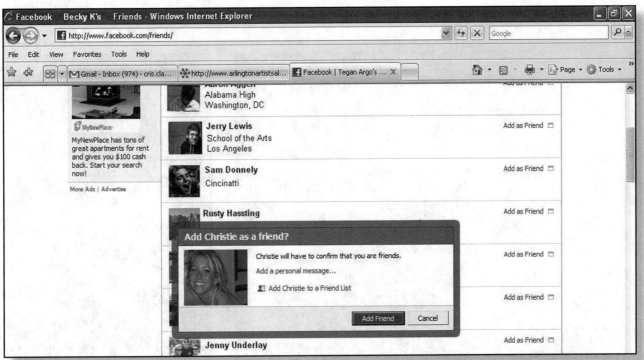

Risky Behavior

> "One of the most important questions to ask that teens really understand [is]: 'Are you willing to share this information in front of your school assembly?' Have a discussion with them [about] what's appropriate and what's not. Look at their images and see if you think [there's] something that shouldn't be on the profile and then have them either remove it or let us know you're concerned and then we'll work with you."
>
> ♂ Hemanshu Nigam
> Chief Security Officer
> Fox Interactive Media
> and MySpace

In the offline world, communities are typically responsible for enforcing norms of privacy and general etiquette. In the online world, new etiquette challenges abound. In order to reap the benefits of socializing and making new friends, teens often disclose information about themselves that would typically be part of an acceptable "getting-to-know-you" process *offline* (name, school, personal interests, etc.). On social network sites, this kind of information is now posted *online*—sometimes in full public view. In some cases, this information is innocuous or fake. But in other cases, disclosure reaches a level that is troubling for parents and those concerned about the safety of online teens, and once children put this information online, they will never get it back.

Since kids are often trying to catch the attention of and gain approval from their peers, some teens tend to post content to appear popular or to gain a response from others in their online community; teens jockey for status, post risqué pictures, brag about the previous weekend's adventures, and can easily use this digital space to humiliate others or post inappropriate content.[5] *No information is truly private in the online world; an online "friend" can forward any information posted on your child's site in a moment.*

For more information on Social Networking, see EIE's Social Networking Policy (Appendix A-38) or visit **www.connectsafely.org** ▦

To see a more complete listing of risky online behaviors, visit Segment 2, *Predators 101*.

[5] Rosen, Christine. "Virtual Friendship and the New Narcissism." The New Atlantis, Summer 2007.

Unhealthy Online Groups

Unfortunately, although teens can join online groups that are affirming, educational, or entertaining, they can also become part of online groups that are destructive and dangerous. In the online world, kids can encounter peer groups focused on hate, racism, bombs, gangs, drugs, gambling, terrorism, and cults, some of which may try to recruit children and force them to participate in activities that are illegal and dangerous.

Kids can also be exposed to groups that support or fuel behaviors like self-mutilation, anorexia, or even suicide. These groups include "how-to" information that can encourage your child to engage in these actions. ▉

III Online Gaming

> "Online gaming devices are just like a computer, and a lot of parents don't realize that...there are messaging, chat and IM [features]. Using an Xbox, you can receive messages from any of the major platforms like Yahoo text messaging, MSN Messenger and Hotmail. Even if you're in the game, somebody who has your game ID or screen name can send a text message to you and it will pop up on the screen and you can chat just like you do on a computer."
>
> ♂ Chad Gallagher
> Child Exploitation Squad
> FBI

Remember when games were played outside and Pac Man was considered high-tech? Today, it is difficult to distinguish the visuals in an online game from real life. Kids no longer need to go to the arcade to play video games against other kids. The web allows children to play video games with friends around the block or strangers around the world. Kids and adults from all over the globe can now convene in cyberspace to compete in online martial arts matches or band together for a fantasy quest. But, as games become more realistic and playing partners can be anonymous strangers, several concerns have emerged of which parents should be aware.

A) What is online gaming?

Children see the online gaming world as a virtual playground.[6] Gaming consoles operate much in the same way as a computer—children can log online, put on a headset, turn on a webcam, and talk to and play with any of the millions of gamers around the world. Many online games have associated online communities, making online games a form of social activity beyond single-player games.

B) Gaming dangers and concerns

1) Violence

2) Sexual content

   a) Pornography embedded in games (i.e., Grand Theft Auto)

   b) Virtual sex games (allows users to act out sexual fantasies and to participate in voyeuristic sex)

3) Predators

4) Cyberbullies

5) Privacy issues

6) Age-appropriate content

7) Webcams

8) Voice-masking technology

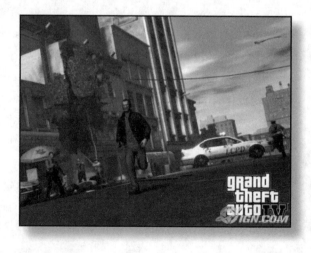

---

[6] <http://en.wikipedia.org/wiki/Online_gaming>.

C) Gaming safety

Setting ground rules at home is essential, but remember, your kids can play games from a friend's computer, an Internet café, and even on mobile devices like iPhones and Blackberries. To help protect your children at home, talk to them about the dangers of online gaming, be ready to listen if they seem upset about something that happened while they were on the computer, and encourage them to use wisdom when deciding what types of online games to play. You can help keep your child's gaming experiences safe, age-appropriate, friendly, fun, and even educational by educating yourself about the gaming community, game ratings, and how to use the privacy and safety tools built into the games. Check out the safety features and parental controls offered by all the major gaming consoles including Xbox, Wii, PlayStation 2 and 3, and mobile gaming devices.

VOICE-MASKING TECHNOLOGY
Did You Know…

Many popular games allow users to disguise their voices. As entertaining as interactive gaming can be, parents should be aware that their children can speak using their own voice with strangers online. Police say predators use this feature to make themselves sound like teenagers. More sophisticated voice changers can make an older man sound like a young boy.

TIPS

Teach your child to:

1) Use voice chat wisely

2) Be aware of voice _____ technology

3) Use suitable screen names (gamertags)

4) Be aware of cyberbullies (griefers)

As a parent:

1) Use parental controls on all gaming devices

2) Review games and ratings before buying

3) Disallow webcam use while gaming

4) Set time limits

5) Know who your child is playing with

6) Talk to your child about coming to you if anyone bullies them, asks them for inappropriate pictures or makes them feel uncomfortable

TIPS: TEACH YOUR CHILD TO
ANSWERS:
2) masking

"*Some of the games have an instant messenger feature and you don't know who's on that...it could be anyone. Some of them are role-playing games where you play a character, but there may be 2,000 characters on the same [game]...like a community...so you're talking with them, and that's a good place for sexual predators because you wouldn't expect a 50-year-old to be on that game.*"

♂ Augey, Age 17

GAMING AND WEBCAMS
Parent Alert!

Today, many gaming consoles come equipped with webcams that allow for real-time chat and instant video between online gamers. This is an attractive feature for kids who are gaming with friends or family members, whether across the street or across the country. Unfortunately, predators use this technology as a tool to groom and exploit youth.

With gaming webcam technology, a predator and child can see and talk to each other virtually while playing, using face-to-face time to deepen the online relationship. A seasoned predator will also use the webcam to gain a full view of your home, which may contain identifiable information. For these reasons, Enough Is Enough recommends that webcams be disallowed or only used with strict caution and under close parental supervision.

Online Gaming—A Closer Look

The gaming world is incredibly diverse: some games are free, some are not; some are rated, some aren't; some require subscriptions; others, a one-time fee. Some games have side chat rooms (many with voice chat), most free games ask for an e-mail address (never a good idea for a child!), and all multiplayer games require screen names or character names (called gamertags). Time spent playing games—especially online and multiplayer games—now rivals the amount of time kids watch TV.

Parents can't assume that their kids are safe when they are playing games online. With the violence related to online gaming increasing, it is important for parents to know if their kids are involved in online gaming. Parents should talk to their kids about what they are doing online as well as a computer-savvy friend if they need help determining if their kids are "gamers." ▪

Sex & Gaming

A key concern about the popularity of video games is that so much of the content is hypersexualized. Pornography is often embedded in these games, allowing kids to engage in virtual or simulated sex acts to accumulate more points. The images of males and females depicted in these games are also often overtly sexual, and many games glorify violence and sexual exploitation.

Some games exist for the sole purpose of simulating sex—virtual sex games are often free and easy to access for kids; these games allow kids to create an online identity to explore sexuality in any place and in any way, including group sex, bestiality, and other fetishes. ■

> "Parents need to understand [how] intricately linked the gaming industry and pornography industry are...more and more games have pornography embedded in them...if they play games online, that is a pornographer's heyday for marketing, grooming and hooking young consumers."
>
> ♀ Jill Manning, Ph.D.
> Marriage and Family
> Therapist

| A CLOSER LOOK |

"Predators use gaming very similar to the way they're using social networking information in chat. They're able to go online and get a lot of information without even talking to you, just looking at your profile, looking at the types of games you play, when you play. They could figure out when you're home and where you are."

♂ Chad Gallagher
Child Exploitation Squad
FBI

Predators & Gaming

Children are often instantly drawn to the realistic images and fast-paced action online gaming has to offer. A first-person shootout or a high-stakes poker match gives a jolt of sensation that can become quite addictive. But, since predators prey where kids play, it is no surprise that online games are the new frontier for sexual predators. They use online gaming to connect with children and groom and target their next victim.

Online gaming allows predators to build shared online experiences and be a child's defender or online teammate. Anyone has access to a wealth of information about a child by viewing a child's gaming history. In so doing, predators have all the information they need to build trust and camaraderie in a way unique to gaming platforms.

Parents should become familiar with parental control features located on the game console that restricts who has access to a child's gaming profile and allows parents to decide what games their kids can play, with whom they play and talk, and when they play online games. ▪

Predators use gaming consoles to 'get foot in the door.'

- In the spring of 2008, a man in Utah was charged with sexual exploitation of a minor for enticing a 12-year-old boy he met through an online game into having sex.

- In December 2007, Michigan prosecutors convicted Adam Glenn Schroeder of criminal sexual conduct with a minor and using a computer to commit a crime. He used World of Warcraft to lure a 12-year-old girl into having sex with him. He was sentenced to ten years in prison.

- In another case, a ten-year-old boy playing the Halo Xbox game got a video message from a man that showed adults engaged in a sex act.[7]

- In 2007, the FBI arrested a 30-year-old Dayton, Ohio, woman who allegedly used an Xbox 360 to send naked pictures of herself to a 16-year-old in Arizona. Police said she then was able to persuade the teen to send her naked pictures of him.[8]

[7] Koch, Wendy. "Predators use gaming consoles to 'get foot in the door.'" USA Today. 2 July 2008. <http://www.usatoday.com/tech/news/ 2008-07-01_porn_N.htm>.

[8] "Video Games New Frontier for Sexual Predators." WAPT.com News (ABC). 1 May 2008.

Ⅳ Cyberbullying

Gone are the days when a child's home is a refuge from playground or neighborhood bullies. The Internet is the new playground, and there are no off-hours. Tech-savvy students are turning to cyberspace to harass their peers using a new method of bullying—cyberbullying.

A) What is cyberbullying and how prevalent is it?

1) Cyberbullying is willful and repeated harm (i.e., harassing, humiliating, or threatening text or images) inflicted through the Internet, interactive technologies, or mobile phones.

2) Kids are being bullied online at alarming rates:

> ▣ *43% of teens aged 13 to 17 report that they have experienced some sort of cyberbullying in the past year.*[9]

B) Cyberbullying tactics

1) Gossip
Posting or sending cruel gossip to damage a person's reputation and relationships with friends, family, and acquaintances

2) Exclusion
Deliberately excluding someone from an online group

3) Impersonation
Breaking into someone's e-mail or other online account and sending messages that will cause embarrassment or damage to the person's reputation and affect his or her relationship with others

4) Harassment
Repeatedly posting or sending offensive, rude, and insulting messages

5) Cyberstalking
Posting or sending unwanted or intimidating messages, which may include threats

> *"A child says something maybe not being very sensitive to the other. The other child gets really angry, comes back and that's how it all grows...It's all related to the fact that this is online and they wouldn't say that face-to-face because they would immediately recognize that they hurt somebody's feelings."*
>
> ♀ Nancy Willard, Director
> Center for Safe and
> Responsible Internet Use
> Internet Use

[9] <http://www.harrisinteractive.com/news/newsletters/k12news/HI_TrendsTudes_2007_v06_i04.pdf>.

☚ ADDITIONAL CYBERBULLYING TACTICS NOT MENTIONED IN VIDEO INCLUDE:

○ **Flaming:** Online *fights* where scornful and offensive messages are posted on websites, forums, or blogs

○ **Outing and Trickery:** Tricking someone into revealing secrets or embarrassing information, which is then shared online

○ **Cyberthreats:** Remarks on the Internet threatening or implying violent behavior, displaying suicidal tendencies

Cyberbullying Resources

- http://cyberbully.org
- http://cyber-safe-kids.com
- http://www.stopcyber bullying.com/

C) Impact of cyberbullying

1) Cyberbullying victims experience the same negative effects as those bullied "offline" (low self-esteem, depression, anger, school failure and avoidance, and in some cases, school violence or suicide) but often to a much larger degree[10] since messages can be made public online for an unlimited audience to view.

2) There is no escape from those who are being cyberbullied—kids can be bullied anytime, anywhere.

D) Cyberbullying safety tips for children

Teach your child to:

1) Follow the Golden Rule: "Do unto others as you would have them do unto you."

2) Talk to you if anyone makes them feel uncomfortable or threatened.

3) Avoid posting anything they wouldn't want their worst enemy to know.

4) Try and stay calm—if someone bullies them online, they do not need to respond.

[10] Willard, Nancy. Educator's Guide to Cyberbullying and Cyberthreats. Center for Safe and Responsible Use of the Internet (2005-07). <http://cyberbully.org/cyberbully/docs/cbcteducator.pdf>.

"If We Only Knew, If He Only Told Us"
Parents of Ryan Halligan

Thirteen-year-old Ryan Halligan was repeatedly bullied in school by his middle school classmates who used the Internet to spread vicious rumors, taunt, and threaten him. Ryan could never seem to escape his bullies—even within the walls of his own home. Tragically, in 2003, the Vermont teen took his own life. Following his death, Ryan's parents discovered a folder filled with IM ex-changes and e-mails between Ryan and his classmates, and they realized technology was being utilized as a weapon far more effective and pervasive than the simple bullying tactics they had encountered as kids. All the while, *Ryan's parents thought they knew all the risks the Internet posed and believed they had done all they could to protect their child online.*

"The key to addressing cyberbullying will be getting to the parents of the bystander kids, those kids who are not actively involved with this but they are witnessing it. If those competent kids of caring parents can be encouraged to say 'stop, that's not okay. This isn't the way you treat people' to a peer, that is going to be far more effective than any adult intervention."

♀ Nancy Willard, Director, Center for Safe and Responsible Internet Use

Cyberbullying—A Closer Look

The popularity of instant messaging, e-mail, web pages, text messaging, and blogging means that kids are potential targets—all day, every day. Victimization on the Internet through cyberbullying is increasing in frequency and scope. Electronic bullies can remain "virtually" anonymous. Temporary e-mail accounts and pseudonyms in chat rooms, instant messaging programs, and other Internet venues can make it very difficult for adolescents to determine the identity of aggressors. Individuals now have the ability to hide behind some measure of anonymity when using their personal computer or cellular phone to bully another individual.

Talk to your children about cyberbullying:

1) Tell your children they do not have to accept any online activity meant to intimidate, threaten, tease, or harm them or anyone else. Remind them that giving bullies attention is exactly what they want, so ignore them as much as possible. Tell them not to erase or delete messages from cyberbullies. Your children do not have to read the messages they receive from bullies, but they (or you) need to keep messages as evidence. To report cyberbullying, it is important to save as much information as possible. The more you save, the easier it will be to track down the people that are bothering your child. (Save the e-mail, e-mail address, date and time received, copies of all relevant e-mails, screenshots, etc.).

Finally, use software to block bullies if encountered through chat or IM and use privacy settings on social networking pages.

2) Encourage your children to talk to you if anybody says or does something online that makes them feel uncomfortable or threatened. It's important to stay calm and keep open lines of communication with your children. Make sure you or your children tell their school if the bullying is school related or involves another student. If you or your children are threatened with harm, contact your local police.

3) Watch for the warning signs of being cyberbullied, such as reluctance to use the computer, a change in your child's behavior and mood, or reluctance to go to school.

4) Tell your children to guard their contact information. Children should assume that people <u>will</u> use the information they post online to cause them harm. Remind your children that the people they communicate with and befriend online have open access to ALL of their posted content and information, and they can forward or use any of that information against them.

5) Remind your children that those who bully want to make their victims feel as if there is something wrong with them, but victims should know that there is <u>nothing</u> wrong with them; it is the bullies who have the real problem. ▪▪

WEB 2.0 RULES OF ENGAGEMENT

With the unlimited access a child has to the Internet from a variety of computer-based, mobile, and gaming devices, it is essential that parents stay on top of their child's online use. One of the simplest ways to engage your child in a non-threatening way is to open up a dialogue about his or her online experiences.

Ask questions such as:

1) Are your profiles set to private?

2) Would it be easy for someone to track you down?

3) How many online "friends" do you have?

4) What kind of information do you consider safe? Unsafe?

5) Have you posted anything that you wouldn't want your school assembly to see?

6) What messages do your pictures and postings portray?

7) Have you been contacted by a stranger?

8) Have your friends ever put themselves at risk? If so, what did you do about it?

9) Have you ever said or posted anything online you wish you could take back?

10) Has anyone ever hurt your feelings by anything they posted about you online?

Information you glean about your child's online use will help to ensure a safer online environment for your child. See Enough Is Enough's *Rules 'N Tools®* Internet safety guidelines for further information. ⏹

Discussion Questions

> What are some of the specific things parents should know and do to protect their kids on social networking sites?

> How can parents—who often feel overwhelmed with new technology—talk to their kids about social networking sites? What are some questions they can ask?

> What should parents do if they are concerned their child might be a victim of cyberbullying?

> What are some of the big concerns about allowing children to participate in online gaming?

How Cyber Savvy Are You?

1. Which of the following Internet-enabled devices are used by the Web 2.0 generation of kids?
a) Cell phones
b) PDAs
c) Gaming devices
d) All of the above

2. Social networking sites are online communities allowing users to:
a) Chat
b) Share their life experiences in an online journal known as a "blog"
c) Display personal information in areas called "profiles"
d) All of the above

3. How can parents find out if their child has a social networking profile?
a) Use the search tool of the social networking site in question

b) Ask you child if he or she has a profile
c) Type you child's name into a search engine such as Google
d) All of the above

4. Which of the following are dangers that can result through the use of social networking sites?
a) A child can lie about his or her age and gain access onto the site
b) A child can post inappropriate pictures and videos
c) Predators and cyberbullies can have easy access to their victims
d) All of the above

5. Which of the following can be cause for concerns regarding online gaming?
a) Violent and/or sexual content
b) Webcam use
c) The use of voice-masking technology
d) All of the above

6. Which is NOT a tactic cyberbullies use to taunt their intended target?
a) Gossip
b) Impersonation
c) Harassment
d) Blogging
e) Cyberstalking

7. I can better protect my child while using the mobile devices such as cell phones, iPhones, Blackberrys, and PDAs, by:
a) Disabling or limiting text messaging
b) Disabling or limiting photo text messaging
c) Disabling or limiting Internet access
d) Disabling or limiting video capabilities
e) All of the above

If you answered all questions correctly, congratulations! You are several steps closer to helping your children become safer online!

Answers: (1) D; (2) D; (3) D; (4) D; (5) D; (6) D; (7) E

An ounce of prevention is worth a pound of cure.

To learn more about protecting your children in the Web 2.0 world, visit the Safety 101 section.

Notes:

_____

_____

_____

_____

_____

_____

_____

_____

_____

_____

_____

_____

_____

_____

_____

_____

_____

_____

_____

SEGMENT 4
SAFETY 101

Introduction to Internet Safety:
Rules 'N Tools®

As you've learned in the previous three segments, despite its many benefits, the Internet also opens children up to significant dangers, and no child is immune. Although Internet safety is a shared responsibility between the public, the Internet industry, and the legal community, significant gaps exist between the Internet's dangers and the level of legal, enforcement-based, and industry-driven action dedicated to protecting children. In this ever-changing world, parents are the first line of defense against child victimization online, shouldering the burden of protecting children from illegal pornography, sexual predators, and emerging Internet threats.

Defending children against these dangers can seem like an overwhelming task. While there is no silver bullet to keep kids safe in the virtual space, the good news is that you don't need a Ph.D. in Internet technology to be a great cyber-parent. However, you *do* need to make a commitment to become familiar with the technology your children use and to stay current with Internet safety issues. In this segment our goal is to educate, empower, and equip you with the basic safety rules and software tools *(Rules 'N Tools®)* you need to know to protect your children online.

> *"You need some rules, you need some tips, [and] you need some tools. They complement one another; one without the other is not the right approach... you have to use them in conjunction with each other, and [with] some common sense."*
>
> ♂ Tim Lordan, Executive Director
> Internet Education Foundation
> and GetNetWise

Encourage Critical Thinking

Help your children to think critically about their online activities and prepare them to make good choices on the Internet. Stimulate discussion, role-play different safety scenarios with them and ask them what they do to stay safe online and what they can do better!

SEGMENT 4 GOALS:

TO TEACH YOU ABOUT:
- ✔ The basic *Rules 'N Tools*® you need to know to protect children online;
- ✔ Parental controls: how they work and how they keep your kids safe; and
- ✔ Additional technical resources to protect your children on all Internet-enabled devices.

Our Approach

EIE pioneered a three-pronged, preventative approach to create and sustain a safe, entertaining, and informative Internet environment, and to protect kids from online threats by:

1) **Raising public awareness** of the dangers of illegal pornography, sexual predation, and other dangers on the Internet in order to empower and equip parents and other child caregivers to implement safety measures;

2) **Encouraging the technology industry** to implement viable technological solutions and family-friendly corporate policy to reduce online threats; and,

3) **Promoting legal solutions** by calling for aggressive enforcement of existing laws and enactment of new laws to stop the exploitation and victimization of children using the Internet.

The "3 C's"

By implementing *Rules 'N Tools®* on all Internet-enabled devices (including desktop and laptop computers, cell phones, PDAs, and gaming devices) used by your children, you will be able to effectively protect them from the "**3 C's**":

1) Dangerous **Content** such as pornography, violence, racism, drugs, gambling, and gangs;

2) Dangerous **Contact** such as sexual predators, cyberbullies, and identity thieves; and

3) Dangerous **Conduct** including all of the risky behaviors discussed in our first three segments.

EIE's preventative strategy of using both safety rules and software tools for Internet safety has been widely adopted by industry, law enforcement, government, and other Internet safety organizations as the most comprehensive approach to keeping kids safe online!

A report by the National Research Council of the National Academy of Sciences included a compelling metaphor to explain why a combined approach to Internet safety is the most important way to keep kids safe online:

> *Technology—in the form of fences around pools, pool alarms, and locks—can help protect children from drowning in swimming pools. However, teaching a child to swim—and when to avoid pools—is a far safer approach than relying on locks, fences, and alarms to prevent him or her from drowning. Does this mean that parents should not buy fences, alarms, or locks? Of course not—because they do provide some benefit. But parents cannot rely exclusively on those devices to keep their children safe from drowning, and most parents recognize that a child who knows how to swim is less likely to be harmed than one who does not. Furthermore, teaching a child to swim and to exercise good judgment about bodies of water to avoid has applicability and relevance far beyond swimming pools—as any parent who takes a child to a beach can testify.[1]*

An Ounce of Prevention Is Worth a Pound of Cure!

[1] Computer Science and Telecommunications Board, National Research Council. <u>Youth, Pornography, and the Internet</u>. Washington, DC: National Academy Press, 2002. 187.

Video Follow-Along Section

Rules 'N Tools® **Internet Safety Guidelines for Parents, Guardians, and Educators**

Implement both safety rules and software tools to protect children online. Focus on the positives of Internet use, while also teaching your children about the dangers and empowering them to make wise choices online.

INTERNET SAFETY "RULES"
Non-Technical Measures

1) Establish an ongoing _____ and keep lines of communication open

2) Supervise use of all _____ - _____ devices

3) Know your child's online _____ and _____

4) Regularly check the _____ _____ your children use, such as social networking and gaming sites, to see what information they are posting

5) Supervise the _____ and _____ your kids post and send online and through their mobile devices

6) Discourage the use of _____ and mobile video devices

7) Teach your children how to protect _____ information posted online and to follow the same rules with respect to the personal information of others

8) Be sure your children use _____ settings

9) Instruct your child to avoid meeting _____ to _____ with someone they only know online or through their mobile device

10) Teach your child how to respond to _____

11) Establish online _____ (see *Rules 'N Tools®* Youth Pledge) and an agreement with your children about Internet use at home and outside of the home

INTERNET SAFETY "RULES"
NON-TECHNICAL MEASURES
ANSWERS:
 1) dialogue
 2) Internet-enabled
 3) activities and friends
 4) online communities
 5) photos and videos
 6) webcams
 7) personal
 8) privacy
 9) face to face
10) cyberbullies
11) rules

INTERNET SOFTWARE "TOOLS"
Technical Measures (also known as "parental controls")

Parental controls should be used on all Internet-enabled devices (desktops, laptops, and gaming, mobile, and music devices).

1) Set age-appropriate _____

2) Consider using _____ software, especially if you sense your child is at risk

3) Periodically check your child's online activity by viewing your browser's _____

4) Set _____ limits

5) Disallow access to _____ and only allow live audio chat with extreme caution

6) Limit your child's instant messaging (IM) contacts to a parent-approved _____ list

7) Use safe _____ engines

8) Set up the family's cyber- _____ protections

9) Utilize _____ _____ on your child's mobile phone and other mobile devices

INTERNET SOFTWARE "TOOLS"
TECHNICAL MEASURES (ALSO KNOWN AS
"PARENTAL CONTROLS")
ANSWERS:
1) filters
2) monitoring
3) history
4) time
5) chat rooms
6) buddy
7) search
8) security
9) parental controls

Protecting Kids Online: The Basics

Since 1994, Enough Is Enough has been on the front lines of the effort to make the Internet safer for children and families, spearheading educational initiatives, advising industry leaders, testing technical measures, and partnering with organizations and groups across the country to equip parents, educators, and guardians with the best safety solutions available. During this time, Enough Is Enough has found that although technology has evolved substantially, the basics of Internet safety have not significantly changed.

To use a sports analogy: the best coaches often teach their teams the basic plays of the game and train them to execute those plays well. In this segment, we hope to teach you the fundamentals of Internet safety *Rules 'N Tools®* and equip you to implement these basic measures to help you become an "empowered" protector of the children entrusted under your care.

❶ Internet Safety "Rules" (Non-Technical Measures)

Before you even turn on the computer, you can make a positive impact on your child's Internet safety. When parents talk regularly with their kids about the Internet, kids demonstrate fewer risky behaviors while online. By following these non-technical, commonsense measures you will be taking a significant step along the path toward protecting your children online.

◑▶ RULE #1: ESTABLISH AN ONGOING DIALOGUE AND KEEP LINES OF COMMUNICATION OPEN

Spend time online alongside your children and create an atmosphere of trust. Encourage your children to make good choices and temper your reactions when they run into dangers.

■ *Teens whose parents have talked to them "a lot" about online safety are less likely to consider meeting face to face with someone they met on the Internet (**12% vs. 20%**).[2]*

"Talk to your teen about what they do online and you'll be surprised how much they'll have fun sharing with you, because they get to teach you something. And I know the conversations about online safety are effective, because one day, I was sitting in another room and heard my twelve-year-old say to my

"If parents don't use safety rules and appropriate tools to keep their kids and their families safe, some sort of contact or access with a predator is almost inevitable. Your child is going to receive unwanted content and encounter somebody who has ill intent. You have to take those simple basic steps. If you do them, you maximize the likelihood that your child will be safe and [able to] use the Internet for all the wonderful benefits it brings."

♂ Ernie Allen, President & CEO
National Center for Missing &
Exploited Children

[2] Cox Communications Teen Internet Safety Survey, Wave II—in Partnership with the National Center for Missing & Exploited Children. March 2007. <http://www.cox.com/TakeCharge/includes/docs/survey_results_2007. ppt#271,1,Slide 1>.

seven-year-old, 'you're not allowed to talk to anybody online. You don't know who they are.' And I walked into the room to see what was going on, and my seven-year-old was playing a game online and she wanted to chat with some other character online, and my twelve-year-old stepped in."

♂ Hemanshu Nigam
Chief Security Officer
Fox Interactive Media and MySpace

RULE #2: SUPERVISE USE OF ALL INTERNET-ENABLED DEVICES

One of the oldest Internet safety rules is to keep your child's computer in an open area of your home. Now, with the ability to access the Internet on multiple devices including cell phones, portable music devices (MP3 players), gaming devices, and PDAs, parents must be just as vigilant, if not more so, about supervising all of their child's Internet access points.

"The Internet is no longer tied to wires and a PC sitting on a desk in your living room. It's now in your child's cell phone, it's in the PDA, it's in these other devices. Parents need to be smart, knowledgeable and aware and make sure that they empower their children to understand [the risks] before they happen."

♂ Ernie Allen
President & CEO
National Center for Missing & Exploited Children

Did You Know...

Skype™ is a popular computer program that enables users to set up profiles, make free phone calls; and chat and video chat through their computer or mobile device from any point around the world. This free service functions through a "peer-to-peer" network, which allows individuals to communicate directly with each other rather than through a central server. Since the conversations and content exchanged through Skype are not scrutinized by monitors, children are at risk of exposure to inappropriate material and dangerous people.

RULE #3: KNOW YOUR CHILD'S ONLINE ACTIVITIES AND FRIENDS

Be familiar with each of your children's passwords, screen names, and all account information, and have them provide the identities of every person on their buddy list or anyone they have "friended" on a social networking or gaming site. Be proactive. Role-play various scenarios your children could encounter online, and remind them that the people they meet online may not be who they say they are. Caution your children to only communicate with people they know in person and whom you have approved.

- *Almost **1 in 8 teens** discovered that someone they were communicating with online was an **adult pretending to be much younger**.*[3]

[3] Internet Safety: Realistic Strategies & Messages for Kids Taking More and More Risks Online. Polly Klaas Foundation. 2006.

"Just be aware of what they're looking at. They can be sitting there looking at [computer images] and their parents walk in [and] they'll just click it and minimize it. Come up [to the computer screen] and look on the bottom of the tool bar and see what they're looking at."

♂ Dustin, Age 18

☾➤ RULE #4: REGULARLY CHECK THE ONLINE COMMUNITIES YOUR CHILDREN USE, SUCH AS SOCIAL NETWORKING AND GAMING SITES, TO SEE WHAT INFORMATION THEY ARE POSTING

Make sure you, as the parent, are added to your child's "friend list," because if their profiles are set to private (as they should be!), you will not be able to view any of their information. If you are unsure whether your child has a profile, conduct a simple online search through the site or by typing their name into a search engine (e.g., Google). Be aware of not only what your children are posting, but what other kids are posting about your children.

"Some of my friend's parents have a MySpace [page], just so they can check on their kids, and their kids don't know about it. I think it's better because some of the kids put on there what they're doing, drinking pictures, or like, 'this is me stoned.' So [their parents] just go on there weekly to check on their kids, and if there's anything wrong with them, then they can deal with it like that."

♂ Augey, Age 17

RULE #5: SUPERVISE THE PHOTOS AND VIDEOS YOUR KIDS POST AND SEND ONLINE AND THROUGH THEIR MOBILE DEVICES

Photos and videos can be uploaded instantly to sites like YouTube and Facebook from any platform with Internet access including your child's cell phone, webcam, PDA, and gaming device. The images your child posts may make them vulnerable to online predators, cyberbullies, strangers, or lead to damaged reputations. Check with your child's school to ensure that any projects, artwork, or photos placed on the school website are only accessible by password (or through the school's intranet) and do not contain any personally identifiable information. Younger children should not post, text or send photos or videos.

■ **4% of all youth** Internet users in 2005 said online solicitors asked them for **nude or sexually explicit photographs** of themselves.[5]

"Some predators will search through various [social networking] pages and look for provocative photos, and they will identify their potential victims in that manner."

♀ Melissa Morrow
Supervisory Special Agent
Child Exploitation Squad
FBI

""My 14-year-old daughter [and I] have had some long conversations about a couple of images she has posted because they have crossed—as my son noted—'Mom's Line.' Young girls—especially—have a very difficult time because they look at all of the images they see and say, 'hey, I can do that.' I have had my rounds with my daughter. 'That picture has to come off.' And sometimes, she says, 'but it's not as bad as the pictures other girls have posted!' Now, if my very savvy daughter has difficulty figuring out where those boundaries are, I think a lot of girls have problems figuring our where those boundaries are. We've got to help young people learn when they're posting images that could attract inappropriate attention."

♀ Nancy Willard
Director, Center for Safe and Responsible Internet Use

[5] Wolak, Janis, Kimberly Mitchell, and David Finkelhor. <u>Online Victimization of Youth: Five Years Later</u>. Alexandria, Virginia: National Center for Missing & Exploited Children, 2006.

RULE #6: DISCOURAGE THE USE OF WEBCAMS AND MOBILE VIDEO DEVICES

Most computers, cell phones and other mobile devices now come with built-in video and webcam devices, but webcams and videos should only be used under close parental supervision or not at all. Videos should only be sent to trusted friends and family. Never allow a webcam or mobile video device to be used by your child in his or her bedroom or other private areas.

"My recommendation to parents whose children want to use a webcam [is] don't let them do it! With the webcam, the person on the other side of that webcam is actually getting a full view of your home. They can see your child. They can see what's in the background that's identifiable, [and] they are taking notice."

♀ Holly Hawkins
Director, Policy and Regulatory Division
America Online

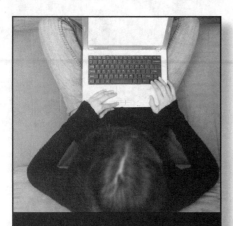

What sort of information is 'Personal'?

Caution your children about posting:

Personal or Contact Information: Your child's full name, address, phone number, passwords, and financial information should only be provided on a secure site and under parental supervision.

Intimate Personal Information: Private, personal, and sensitive information (such as a teen's journal) should not be posted and should only be shared in private e-mails with a trusted personal friend.[7]

Reputation-Damaging Information or Images: Inappropriate pictures (i.e., content that is explicit, suggestive, illegal, etc.), should never be posted or sent.[8]

Event Information: Teach children to use caution when posting information about parties, events, or activities where someone could track them down.

---

[6] Cox Communications Teen Internet Safety Survey.

[7] Willard, Nancy E., Cyber-Safe Kids, Cyber-Savvy Teens. Jossey-Bass, 2007.

[8] Ibid.

RULE #7: TEACH YOUR CHILDREN HOW TO PROTECT PERSONAL INFORMATION POSTED ONLINE AND TO FOLLOW THE SAME RULES WITH RESPECT TO THE PERSONAL INFORMATION OF OTHERS

Remind your children to *think before they post; there are no take-backs online*. Nothing is truly private on the Internet; any and all information sent or posted online is public or can be made public.

◼ *Teens whose parents have talked to them "a lot"* about Internet safety are **more concerned about the risks** of sharing personal information online. For instance, **65% of teens** whose parents have not talked to them about online safety post information about where they live compared to **48% of teens** with more involved parents.[6]

"You never know when something can be passed from one friend to another so be careful about those things and remember, you may be going to college. Colleges are looking at your MySpace page. You may, one day, want to get a job somewhere. Employers are often looking at your MySpace page. So it's always important to remember if you're not willing to do it in the physical world in front of a school assembly, don't do it online."

♂ Hemanshu Nigam
Chief Security Officer
Fox Interactive Media and MySpace

 Remember: Teach your kids that there are no "take-backs" on the Internet!

☛ RULE #8: BE SURE YOUR CHILDREN USE PRIVACY SETTINGS

Privacy settings limit who can view your teen's profiles. On most social networking and gaming sites, your teen can change his or her privacy setting by clicking on "account settings." Ask your teen to show you their account settings or, if you have access to their account, then you can check the settings for yourself. Remember that no one can detect a disguised predator, and even using these settings does not always achieve true privacy: all of your teen's friends have access to and could distribute any material included on the profile.

■ *47% of teens have an Internet profile that is public and viewable by anyone.*[9]

"Even before you add them [to your online "friends"], you can message them. Every time someone tries to add me—if I don't know them, or their picture doesn't look familiar to me, I always message them saying, 'Do I know you?' or, 'Have I seen you before?' If they say, 'No, I just think you're cool,' I'm like 'DENY!' I put [my profile] on private so only my friends can [see it]."

♂ Augey, Age 17

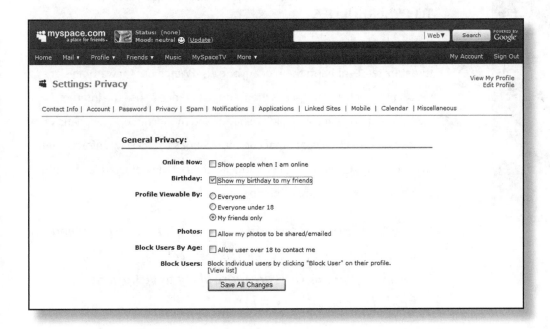

Exhibit 1. An example of MySpace's privacy setting.

(Screen capture as of September 10, 2008)

[9] Willard, Nancy E., Cyber-Safe Kids, Cyber-Savvy Teens. Jossey-Bass, 2007.

☞ RULE #9: INSTRUCT YOUR CHILDREN TO AVOID MEETING FACE TO FACE WITH SOMEONE THEY ONLY KNOW ONLINE OR THROUGH THEIR MOBILE DEVICE

Online and mobile "friends" may not be who they say they are. Children should be advised to come to you if anyone makes them feel scared, uncomfortable, confused, asks for any personal or personally identifiable information, or suggests meeting them.

■ *16% of teens* say they've **considered meeting face-to-face** with someone they've talked to only online, and **8% of teens** say they **have actually met in person** with someone from the Internet.[10]

"I remember opening the door, and feeling the wind bite my face, and being at the top of the hill hiding behind a tree. The very next thing I know, I was in the car, and he was squeezing my hand so tight that I thought it was broken and he said, 'Be good. Be quiet. I've got the trunk cleared out for you.'"

♀ Alicia Kozakiewicz
Teenage victim of online predator and
NCMEC Courage Award Recipient (2007)

☞ RULE #10: TEACH YOUR CHILDREN HOW TO RESPOND TO CYBERBULLIES

Children do not have to accept any online activity meant to intimidate, threaten, tease, or harm them or anyone else. Watch out for warning signs including reluctance to go to school and reluctance to use the Internet; be aware of a change in your child's behavior and mood. Report any offensive or dangerous e-mail, chat, or other communications to local law enforcement. Do not delete the evidence. Remind your child of the golden rule: do unto others as you would have them do unto you.

■ *Overall,* **19% of teens** *report they have been* **harassed or bullied online***, and the incidence of online harassment is higher* **(23%)** *among 16- and 17-year-olds.* **Girls are more likely to be harassed or bullied** *than boys (21% vs. 17%).*[11]

For more information about cyberbullying, see *The Evolving Internet: Web 2.0* **section.**

---

[10] Cox Communications Teen Internet Safety Survey.

[11] Ibid.

RULE #11: ESTABLISH AN AGREEMENT WITH YOUR CHILDREN ABOUT INTERNET USE AT HOME AND OUTSIDE OF THE HOME

(See Appendix A-18 for the Rules 'N Tools® Youth Pledge)

Remind your child that rules for good behavior do not change just because they're on a computer. Post the agreement near the computer. Be willing to sign a parent pledge as well.

"Jack's Box": A Word from Donna Rice Hughes on a "Carrot & Stick" Approach to Online Safety

I'm often asked how I make my own family's experience online a safe one. Our children are now grown, but, while they were under our roof, my husband, Jack, and I instituted our own house rules for behavior both online and off. To teach our children how to conduct themselves responsibly, Jack used the following word picture to help them visualize the concept. It goes something like this:

"Picture your life as operating inside a box. As you consistently demonstrate increasing levels of personal responsibility, the box gets larger, and your world of opportunity increases. When you do not act responsibly, the box shrinks, and we start over again. As the parent responsible for training you in the right way to live, I control the box. At a point in the future, when you have reached adulthood, I expect to turn the control of your box over to you."

In regard to Internet use, as children comply with general safety practices, and your specific house rules established in the *Rules 'N Tools®* Youth Pledge, their freedoms may be expanded; i.e., their "box" of privileges grows. With violations and broken trust, their "box" shrinks and their Internet and computer privileges are restricted.

Review the 4 W's of "Rules": What, Where, When, and Why with your child:[12]

1) **What** type of content is appropriate. For example, "No MTV.com videos."

2) **Where** Internet use is allowed in the home or other locations. For example, "No online games at your friend's house."

3) **When** during the day the Internet is used and for how long. For example, "No Internet on a school night."

4) **Why** you set your rules and their outcomes. For example, "We're limiting your social networking activities until your grades improve."

[12] Thierer, Adam. <u>Parental Controls and Online Protection: A Survey of Tools and Methods</u>. The Progress and Freedom Foundation. 2008. <http://www.pff.org/parentalcontrols/Parental%20Controls%20&%20Online%20Child%20Protection%20%5BVERSION%203.0%5D.pdf>.

Internet Software "Tools" (Technical Measures)

In addition to safety rules, protecting kids online requires the use of software tools, better known as parental controls. These tools are technical measures that allow parents, guardians, and educators to restrict, tailor, or manage Internet content and activity. Parental controls should be utilized on all Internet-enabled devices including desktops, laptops, cell phones, PDAs, and gaming and music devices. However, these resources are not a substitute for parental supervision.

"You can give children all the rules that you can possibly think of, 'Don't go to these sites; don't talk to strangers,' but you need parental controls because they can inadvertently come across [inappropriate content]. They can be sent an e-mail with a link that looks benign and you click on it and see pornography, so parental controls are a necessity."

♀ Holly Hawkins
Director, Policy and Regulatory Division
America Online

TOOL #1: SET AGE-APPROPRIATE FILTERS

Filters block categories of inappropriate websites a child can view such as pornography, violence, gambling, gang activity, and illegal drugs, and settings are password-protected. As we discussed in the *Pornography 101* section, pornographers use many deceptive tactics—such as misspelled words, stealth sites, and pop-up ads—which a good filter can recognize and block. Remember that *filters are not 100% effective* and may not stop a determined child from bypassing them and accessing unsuitable content.

Also, set the filter to block access to peer-to-peer (P2P) networks, which allow users to connect directly to each other's computers to retrieve and swap files, without a server, and which contain tremendous amounts of pornography and child pornography.

■ *7 out of 10* Internet users ages 8 to 18 were **exposed to unwanted sexual material**, and *1 out of 3* youth who viewed pornography, *viewed the pornography intentionally*. More than three-quarters of unwanted exposure to pornography (79%) **happened at home**.[13]

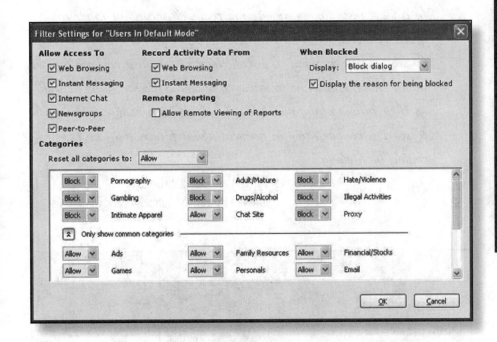

Exhibit 2. An example of filter settings.
(Screen capture as of September 10, 2008)

 Most parental control features include kid-friendly spaces, sometimes referred to as closed systems or "walled gardens." By using these settings, younger children will only be able to access age-appropriate content "within the garden walls."

Do you know the difference between Filtering and Monitoring Tools?

When used together, they provide you with an effective layer of protection.

FILTERING TOOLS:
Allow parents to establish a strong defensive mechanism to prevent children from accidentally encountering or intentionally accessing inappropriate sites.

MONITORING TOOLS:
Allow parents to collect "intelligence" and check up on their child's online activities by tracking a child's website visits, e-mails, instant messaging, and other Internet behavior.

Filter and Monitoring Software Review Sites:

◉ www.child-internet-safety.com

◉ www.monitoringsoftware reviews.org

◉ http://internet-filter-review. toptenreviews.com

◉ www.filterreview.com

◉ www.consumerreports.org

[13] Generation M: Media in the Lives of 8-18 Year-olds. Henry J. Kaiser Family Foundation. 17 Nov. 2006. Wolak, Janis, Kimberly Mitchell, and David Finkelhor. Online Victimization of Youth: Five Years Later. Alexandria, Virginia: National Center for Missing & Exploited Children, 2006.

◐➤ TOOL #2: CONSIDER USING MONITORING SOFTWARE, ESPECIALLY IF YOU SENSE YOUR CHILD IS AT RISK

Monitoring software, or keystroke capture devices, can provide a full and complete record of where your child goes online, monitor outgoing and incoming communications, and identify a child's online buddies. More robust monitoring tools let parents see each website their children visit, view every e-mail or instant message they send and receive, and can even record every word they type. Many monitoring tools can send parents a periodic report summarizing their child's Internet usage and communications.[14] EIE recommends that parents tell their children that monitoring software is being used unless the parent suspects their child is involved in risky behavior, in which case it may be better to go stealth.

■ **80% of sexual predators are explicit** *about their sexual intentions. The offenders lure teens after weeks of online conversations, playing on common teen vulnerabilities such as their desires for romance, adventure, sexual information, and understanding. In* **73% of these crimes, the youth meet the offender on multiple occasions for sexual encounters.**[15]

"In a way, installing a monitoring tool will actually trigger a great conversation with your kids. Maybe you want to start off by saying you're going to install this tool because you really care about them, you want to know their online playgrounds as well as their offline playgrounds, and I think it's a really good way to start a conversation in general about Internet safety that should be lifelong."

♂ Tim Lordan, Executive Director
Internet Education Foundation and GetNetWise

[14] Thierer, Adam. <u>Parental Controls & Online Child Protection</u>.

[15] Finkelhor, David, Kimberly Mitchell, and Janis Wolak. <u>National Juvenile Online Victimization Study</u>. National Center for Missing & Exploited Children, 2007.

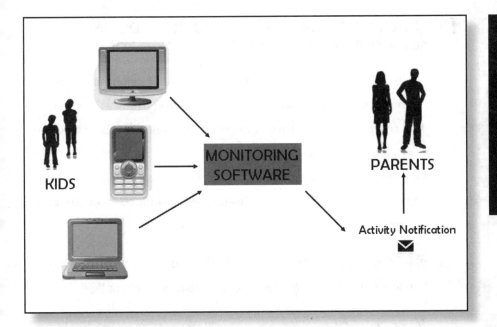

Exhibit 3. How monitoring works.

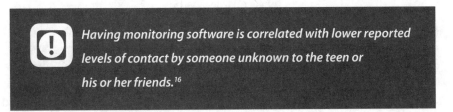

Having monitoring software is correlated with lower reported levels of contact by someone unknown to the teen or his or her friends.[16]

[16] Lenhart, Amanda. Teens, Online Stranger Contact & Cyberbullying: What the research is telling us. Pew Internet & American Life Project, 2008.

Risky Situations: A Word from Nancy Willard

"Now if a child has gotten into a situation where they are being manipulated by someone that is an exceptionally dangerous situation, because that person has likely very effectively interfered with the bonds of the relationship of parents and child and if you think that your child is at risk that would be a time to install monitoring software without telling your child and absolutely do not tell your child. Talk to the local police. I would also immediately talk with a psychologist/counselor to get a safety plan in place for your child before your child knows that you are investigating this because the fact that this relationship now appears to be known could trigger a runaway with this individual. So you've got to have a safety plan, and you need to be working with a professional."

♀ Nancy Willard
Director, Center for Safe and Responsible Internet Use

Exhibit 4. Viewing history through Internet Explorer.

(Screen capture as of September 10, 2008)

Parent Alert!

Your child can easily search the Internet to find resources devoted to instructing them how to disable filtering software and other parental control software, whether at home or school. However, utilizing monitoring software and regularly checking your browser's history can indicate whether your child has made such attempts.

TOOL #3: PERIODICALLY CHECK YOUR CHILD'S ONLINE ACTIVITY BY VIEWING YOUR BROWSER'S HISTORY

Watch out for any sites that sound inappropriate (although, not every inappropriate site has an inappropriate name!). If you notice the history has been cleared or deleted, have a discussion with your child about the sites he or she visited. Be aware that your child may selectively delete files from the history list. If you are concerned about your child's online activity, you may want to install monitoring software. (See "Top 10 Technical Questions" in Appendix B-18.)

■ **65% of all parents** and **64% of all teens** say that teens do things online that they wouldn't want their parents to know about.[17]

"I got caught two times because my parents kept looking at the history thing. They read through it and [saw] 'MySpace, Google, Freakychicks.com' or something like that. And I'd get in trouble."

♂ Kyle, Age 15

TOOL #4: SET TIME LIMITS

Excessive time online, especially at night, may indicate a problem. Remind your child that Internet use is a privilege, not a right. If necessary, utilize time-limiting software tools, which allow parents to manage the amount of time and times of day their children are allowed online.

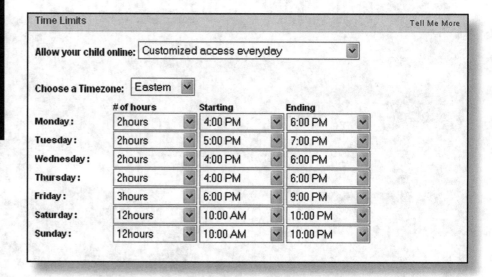

Exhibit 5. Setting time limits through AOL.

[17] Lenhart, Amanda. Family, Friends & Community: Protecting Teens Online. Pew Internet & American Life Project, 2005.

TOOL #5: DISALLOW ACCESS TO CHAT ROOMS AND ONLY ALLOW LIVE AUDIO CHAT WITH EXTREME CAUTION

Chat rooms are the playground of today's sexual predator; they allow immediate, direct communications between participants. Many chat rooms geared toward adolescents are known for explicit sexual talk and obscene language, fostering an atmosphere which may attract online child molesters.[18] Chat rooms also allow users to communicate via webcam and audio chat.

Many gaming programs also come equipped with live audio chat capabilities through which individuals can alter the sound of their voice. Only mature teens should be allowed to use live audio chat. Remind your child to only interact with individuals they know offline. It's impossible for a parent, child, chat room monitor, or any technology tool to recognize a disguised, anonymous predator.

■ ***Most sexual solicitation incidents (79%) happened on home computers***, *beginning with personal questions about the teen's physical appearance, sexual experience and with propositions for "cybersex."* ***37% of sexual solicitation incidents*** *happen while youth* ***are in chat rooms***, *and many occur in live chat or instant-message sessions.*[19, 20]

"There's nothing that a parent can do once a child gets online and gets into a chat room or a website or instant message that can prevent being approached by a predator. So I believe that it has to be proactive instead of reactive, and that's going to require parents to minimize the use of the Internet and really be a parent instead of being a friend."

♂ "John Doe," convicted sex offender

"If I had even the most basic software—software that blocks chat rooms, we may have had a different outcome."

♀ Mary Kozakiewicz
Mother of abducted teenager

[18] Subrahmanyam, Kaveri, David Smahel, and Patricia Greenfield. "Connecting developmental constructions to the Internet: Identity presentation and sexual exploration in online teen chat rooms." Developmental Psychology 42.3 (2006) 395-406.

[19] Wolak, Janis, Kimberly Mitchell, and David Finkelhor, 2006.

[20] Ibid.

Exhibit 6. iChat buddy list.

○→ **TOOL #6:** LIMIT INSTANT MESSAGING (IM) CONTACTS TO A PARENT-APPROVED BUDDY LIST

If you decide to allow your child to use IM, block all communications from anyone not on the child's pre-approved contact list. Robust parental control software will prevent your child from adding anyone to their buddy list unless you have approved the addition. However, since some kids are able to bypass parental controls, regularly check their buddy list to ensure that it has not been altered. Be aware that many online communities such as social networking and gaming sites now have IM and chat features, and not all parental control software provides coverage over these new chat platforms.

"You have to watch who your children are talking to, and know who your children are talking to in a one-on-one conversation. We've given parents parental controls that can actually allow or disallow people to talk to their children through instant messaging."

♀ Holly Hawkins
Director, Policy and Regulatory Division
America Online

◑► TOOL #7: USE SAFE SEARCH ENGINES

Although search engines enable your kids to find fun websites and educational information, they can also be an efficient gateway to pornography and other objectionable content. Major search engines have addressed this need by creating child-safe zones. Some give the option of parental controls or safe searches. Consult the information on your search engine provider to make sure that the safe search is on.

Safe Search Filtering Tools
An example using Google's image search
(Screen capture as of September 10, 2008)

SCREEN SHOT #1

▲ You can adjust the search options by going to the "Search Setting" feature on the right side of the screen.

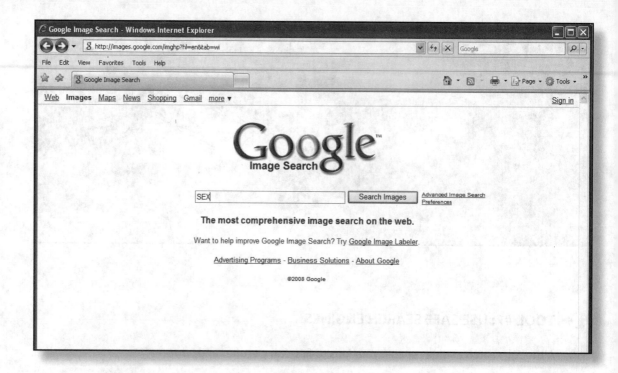

▲ This is an example of a Google image search of the word "sex." In this screen, "sex" is typed into the search engine.

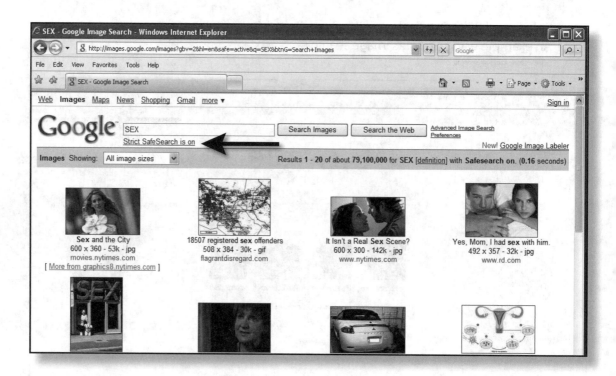

▲ Using the strict search settings, as you can see in the results, the images are mostly wholesome.

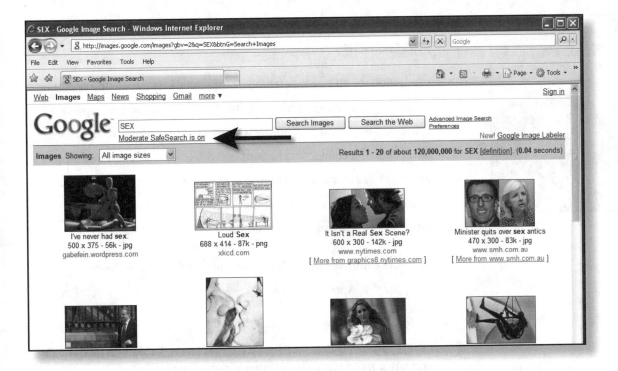

▲ Using the moderate search setting, the images become more racy.

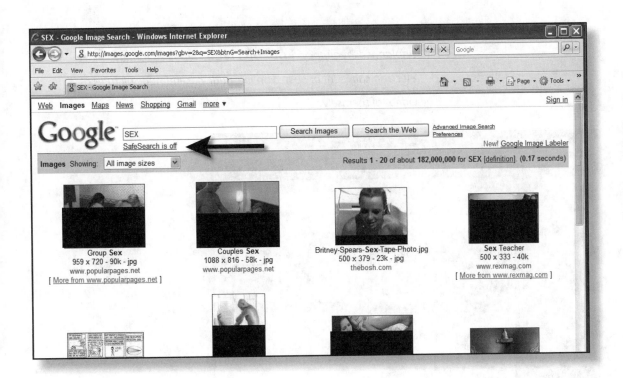

▲ Finally, with the safe search turned off, we had to block most of the images to show you what came up.

TOOL #8: SET UP THE FAMILY'S CYBER-SECURITY PROTECTIONS

In addition to setting up parental controls, regularly update the operating system and install a firewall and up-to-date anti-virus and anti-spyware software. The instant a computer is connected to the Internet or an "always on" broadband connection, hackers and thieves can attempt to gain access to the family's financial and personal information. By securing your computer, you can help protect against Internet intruders and the malicious programs they can use to infiltrate your computer.

For more cyber-security information, see the "Top 10 Technical Questions" in Appendix B-18.

TOOL #9: UTILIZE PARENTAL CONTROLS ON YOUR CHILD'S MOBILE PHONE AND MOBILE DEVICES:

All of the major cell phone carriers offer parental controls of some level, including the ability to set content filters, disable or limit Internet access on Web-enabled phones. Mobile controls can also allow parents to disable, limit or monitor a child's text, picture and video messaging.

☐ *In a recent survey from the National Campaign to Prevent Teen and Unplanned Pregnancy,* **1 out of 5 teens** *reported that they have 'electronically sent or posted online, nude or semi-nude pictures of videos of themselves.'*

Exhibit 7. Symantec Family Safety security protections.

(Screen capture as of September 10, 2008)

Rules 'N Tools® Parent's Pledge

EIE encourages parents to pledge their commitment to implement *Rules 'N Tools®* on all Internet-enabled devices used by their children. Being proactive with online safety is an act of love that will help keep your children safe. (See Appendix A-16 for Enough Is Enough's *Rules 'N Tools®* Parent's Pledge.)

Rules 'N Tools® Parent Buddy Check

Consider enlisting another parent or friend as your "Parent Buddy." The buddy-check system is designed to encourage parents to help each other implement and enforce *Rules 'N Tools®* and to stay current on Internet safety issues. (See Appendix A-17 for *Rules 'N Tools®* Parent Buddy Check.)

"It's hard being a parent in the 21st century. What parents have to do is keep up, listen, and learn. Use the tools and resources that are out there and available because the world is changing fast. Parents need to empower their children, because children who are talked to about the risks they face, and [who] understand, before they happen, the potential risks, are far less vulnerable."

♂ Ernie Allen
President & CEO
National Center for Missing & Exploited Children

Did You Know...
VOICE-MASKING TECHNOLOGY

Many popular games allow users to disguise their voices. As entertaining as interactive gaming can be, parents should be aware that their children can speak using their own voice with strangers online. Police say predators use this feature to make themselves sound like teenagers. More sophisticated voice changers can make an older man sound like a young boy!

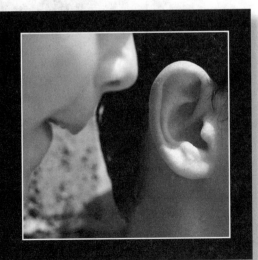

A Closer Look:
Parental Controls

I. What Are Parental Controls?

A) Parental controls are any tools or methods parents might use to restrict, tailor, or manage the media content their children consume. *A comprehensive suite of parental controls should include customizable filters, monitoring software, time-managing controls, and IM and chat controls. These tools should be utilized on all Internet-enabled devices (desktops, laptops, and gaming, mobile, and music devices).*

B) Parental Control tools are available for purchase and to download as separate software packages; through your Internet service provider (ISP); or as software available or pre-loaded with your operating system (i.e., computer).

The following are examples of the different sources of parental controls:

1) **INDEPENDENT TOOLS**

   (e.g., BSafe Online, NetNanny, Safe Eyes, and Symantec)

2) **INTERNET SERVICE PROVIDER (ISP) PROVIDED CONTROLS**

   (e.g., AOL, Verizon)

   a) **Example #1:** AOL's Parental Controls include customizable filters, monitoring software, time-managing controls, and chat and instant messaging controls, available at no cost for AOL and non-AOL users alike.

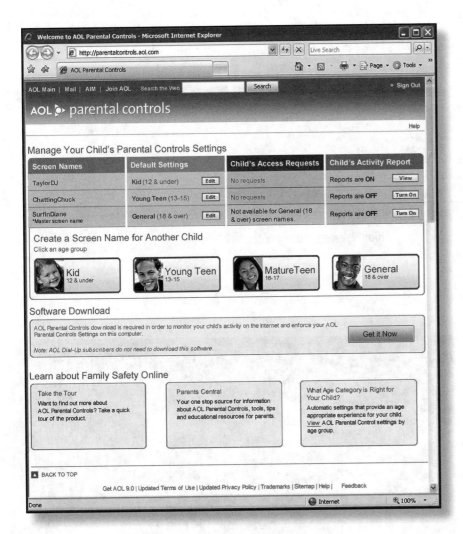

Exhibit 8. AOL's parental controls.

b) Example #2: Verizon also offers an Internet security suite to help identify and block websites that parents decide are inappropriate for their children.

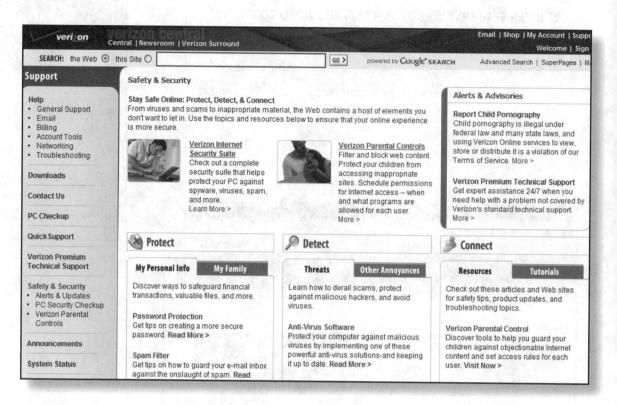

Exhibit 9. Verizon's Internet security suite.

(Screen capture as of September 10, 2008)

3) OPERATING SYSTEMS AND WEB BROWSER CONTROLS

(e.g., Microsoft's Vista; Apple's Leopard)

a) **Example #1: Windows Vista**—Microsoft's operating system incorporates embedded family safety tools for gaming, web browsing, file downloading, and instant messaging.[21] Vista lets parents establish "administrator" accounts by which they can oversee the other user accounts on the family's computer. Parents can also configure the Vista sub-accounts to enable various parental control features and monitoring tools, turn on web filters to block specific types of potentially objectionable website content or downloads, and set time limits that restrict how long a child may use the computer.[22]

Exhibit 10. Operating system, Microsoft Vista's parental controls.

[21] Schiesel, Seth. "For Parents, New Ways to Control the Action," New York Times 7 Jan. 2007. <http://www.nytimes.com/2007/01/08/arts/08vist.html>.

[22] Thierer, Adam. Parental Controls & Online Child Protection.

b) **Example #2: Apple's OS X "Leopard"**— Apple's operating system allows parents to establish accounts for their children and keep tabs on their online activities using monitoring tools and time management controls. In addition, parents can also build a restricted "buddies list" for their children, which disallows instant messaging to anyone not included in the parent-restricted list. The system can also hide the child's online status so that only pre-approved buddies can see that they are online at any time.[23]

Weekday time limits

Allows access to this computer Monday through Friday for the specified number of hours only.

3 hours a day

☐ Limit computer use to:

30 minutes   8 hours

Weekend time limits

Allows access to this computer Saturday and Sunday for the specified number of hours only.

5 hours a day

☐ Limit computer use to:

30 minutes   8 hours

Bedtime

Prevents access to this computer during the specified hours.

☐ **School nights:**   8:00 PM   to   6:00 AM
Sunday – Thursday

☐ **Weekend:**   8:00 PM   to   6:00 AM
Friday and Saturday

Exhibit 11. Operating system, Apple's parental controls, time-limiting features.

23 Ibid.

II. Parental Controls for Mobile Phones

"With regard to rules and tools on your mobile devices, just think of them as no different than a mini little computer or a mini laptop. Parents have to realize that no matter what computer screen or mobile screen their kids are looking at, that's a real world for them and they're having real experiences online, and they're accessing content. Parents have to just come to the realization that there's a lot of things that their children are doing on mobile devices that they should know about."

♂ Tim Lordan
Executive Director
Internet Education Foundation and GetNetWise

Did You Know...

The wireless industry has pledged to "proactively provide tools and controls to manage wireless content offered by the carriers or available via Internet-enabled wireless devices,"[24] so check with your wireless provider to see what resources they have to protect your children.

As we learned in *The Evolving Internet: Web 2.0* section, cell phones have all the capabilities of a personal computer, now able to deliver video, data, games, instant messages, and more. These multi-media platforms allow subscribers "anywhere, anytime" access to information, news, and people, making it more difficult for parents to monitor access, and creating another point of access to inappropriate content and contacts.

[24] CTIA Press Release. "Wireless Carriers Announce 'Wireless Content Guidelines.'" 8 Nov. 2005. <http://www.ctia.org/media/press/body.cfm/prid/1565>.

III. Parental Controls for Wireless Devices

Most major mobile carriers and providers (e.g. Verizon, ATT, iPhone, etc.) offer parental control options. The following are a few examples of carriers that provide parents with customized resources and limits to protect kids on mobile platforms. Check with your provider and carrier to see what options are available for your family.[25]

AT&T ("Smart Limits" and Media Net)—allows parents to determine how and when kids use phones; limit the number of text and instant messages; decide when the phone can be used for calling or texting; and limit access to inappropriate content.

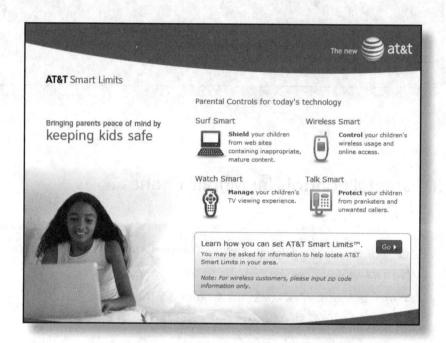

Exhibit 12. AT&T's wireless parental controls.

[25] Thierer, Adam. Parental Controls & Online Child Protection.

A CLOSER LOOK

Verizon Wireless ("Chaperone Services" & "Content Filtering Services")—allows parents to determine their child's location—in real time—and notifies parents if their child leaves the parent-specified "Child Zone." Verizon also offers parents tools which filter content (classified by age); set phone usage allowances; set time restrictions; and block numbers.

Exhibit 13. Verizon's wireless parental controls.

(Screen capture as of September 10, 2008)

Did You Know...

Although GPS technology located within mobile devices can be a helpful tool for parents to use to track their children's whereabouts, for tech-savvy sexual predators, a GPS can also help them to track down a child. By simply hacking into a child's cell phone GPS system, any adult can pinpoint a child's location at any given time. Parents should contact their cell phone service provider to determine the necessary steps to take in order to prevent this from happening.

Sprint—offers phones with built-in Parental Controls, which allow parents to restrict incoming and outgoing calls to a parent-approved contact list (located in the child's phone book), and also offers parents other resources to limit a child's access to all other Sprint services.

Parent Alert! Street View Technology

Street View Technology, available through Google Maps, gives anyone with Internet connectivity the ability to view street level pictures of any address that has been captured in the Street View program. Using these images of thousands of homes, schools, parks and playgrounds from around the country, anyone is able to view unprecedented amounts of information about your family, your children, and your neighborhood, without your permission.

While this technology is very exciting on many fronts, unfortunately, it could make it simple for anyone to map the most likely route a child might walk to school, view images of entrances to community parks, and even find the location of a bedroom window.

For more information, see
www.StopInternetPredators.org

IV. Parental Controls for Game Consoles

Most gaming devices from console producers (Microsoft, Sony, and Nintendo) come with parental controls and family safety settings. These settings allow parents to restrict access to inappropriate games, restrict audio chat use, choose with whom their children play, and limit the amount of time their children play.

 GAMING OPTIONS FOR PARENTS: Offline gaming is the only way for your children to be safe 100% of the time when they play games. If you choose to allow your child's gaming device to be Internet-connected, provide a layer of protection against gaming dangers by using the controls embedded within your gaming consoles.

Parents who allow their children to participate in online gaming should ensure that their children only play with known, trusted acquaintances.[26]

"It's very important to limit your profile [to] the people you know. With Xbox specifically, you can set up a youth profile or an adult profile. A youth profile limits your ability to text message or to use the chat features and the games, which is strongly recommended."

♂ Chad Gallagher
Child Exploitation Squad
FBI

"Some games have an instant messenger feature, and you don't know who's on that instant messenger, it could be anyone, [and they could] start crap if you do something wrong. You could be talking on the instant messenger with them, and that's a good place for sexual predators because you wouldn't expect a 50-year-old to be on that game. So I would tell parents if the game does have an instant messenger, make sure it's [set for] a 10-11 [year old]. Make sure it has a filter somewhere, where if you say a certain thing, if you say bad words, you get kicked off, because some of them do, and it really helps."

♂ Augey, Age 17

[26] Thierer, Adam. Parental Controls & Online Child Protection.

Examples of gaming console parental controls

Microsoft Xbox 360 and the Nintendo Wii consoles allow parents to enter the Entertainment Software Rating Board (ESRB) rating level that they believe is acceptable for their children. Once they do so, no game rated above that level can be played on the console. Microsoft now offers Xbox 360 owners the ability to employ a "Family Timer" feature that allows parents to limit how and when children play games on the console.[27]

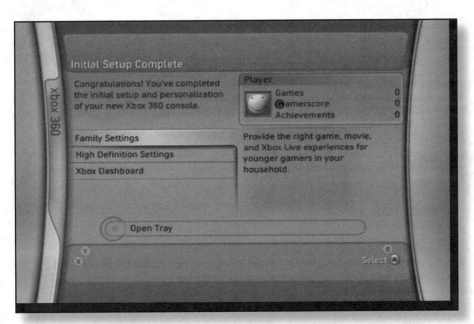

Exhibit 14. Microsoft Xbox parental control set-up menu.

Microsoft now offers a gaming resource **www.GetGameSmart.com** filled with resources, family challenges, and tips to help your family game safely.

Sony's PlayStation 3 and PlayStation Portable systems work a little differently—however, both products let parents use a 1-11 scale to determine the level of game and DVD content they will allow their kids to play. The lower the level, the tighter the restriction.

[27] CTIA Press Release.

| A CLOSER LOOK |

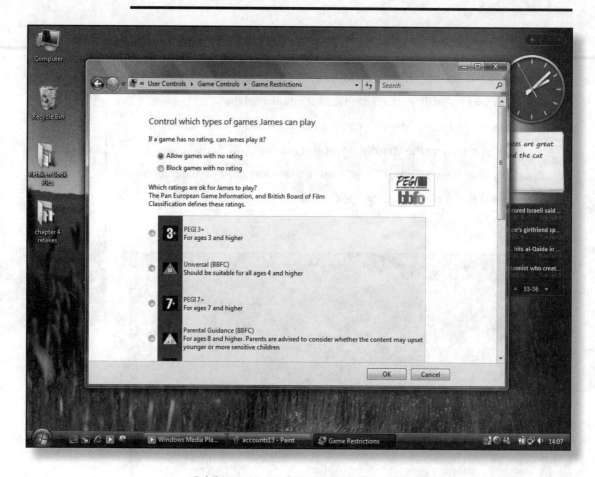

Exhibit 15. Microsoft Vista gaming controls.

Additionally, Microsoft Xbox 360, Sony PS3, and Nintendo Wii allow parents to build the equivalent of a "buddies list" for their kids when using the gaming systems.[28]

 Before children are allowed to access interactive gaming, parents should instruct their children to report any suspicious communications from strangers in these games to the gaming operators.[29]

For more information on online safety, visit www.enough.org. Let us help you protect your children online!

---

[28] Ibid.

[29] Ibid.

Discussion Questions

> Why are parents unable to rely solely on the use of parental controls to protect their children online? Why is it essential for parents to become a part of the safety equation?

> Besides monitoring the use of the home computer, what other Internet-enabled devices do parents need to supervise?

> What are some different types of technical measures parents can take when setting up their Internet service account?

> What are some of the ways the mobile (cell phone) industry has pledged to protect kids while accessing the Internet?

> How have some of the major gaming console producers provided safety measures for children who are involved in online gaming?

> How might the Parent Buddy Check system and Parent's Pledge help you to stay on top of your child's online experiences?

How Cyber Savvy Are You?

1. On which of the following should parents be vigilant about supervising their child's Internet access?

a) Laptop

b) PDA (personal digital assistant)

c) Cell phone

d) All of the above

2. How can parents become familiar with their child's online activities and friends?

a) By knowing their child's passwords

b) By knowing those they are communicating with

c) By asking their child if he or she has "friended" anyone

d) All of the above

3. Which of the following are NOT TRUE regarding the use of webcams?

a) Webcam videos should be only sent to trusted friends and family

b) Webcams should never be used in private areas by your child

c) Younger children do not require parental supervision when using webcams since there is no potential danger associated with their use

d) Webcams now come pre-installed in many computers

4. Which of the following should children be cautious about posting (or not post at all)?

a) Their full name and address

b) Personal information such as a journal

c) Event information such as a location of a party

d) All of the above

5. Some of the potential dangers associated with chat rooms include:

a) Exposure to inappropriate topics

b) Exposure to obscene language

c) Unknowingly interacting with a sexual predator

d) All of the above

6. Which of the following parental controls and features can be used to provide a safer online environment for your child?

a) Monitoring software

b) Filters

c) A and B

d) Blogs (web logs)

7. True or False: Filters and monitoring software are effective substitutes for parental supervision.

If you answered all questions correctly, congratulations! You are several steps closer to helping your children become safer online!

Answers: (1) D; (2) D; (3) C; (4) D; (5) D; (6) C; (7) False

An ounce of prevention is worth
a pound of cure.

Notes:

_____

_____

_____

_____

_____

_____

_____

_____

_____

_____

_____

_____

_____

_____

_____

_____

_____

_____

_____

_____

_____

Internet Safety 101^{SM} Program
FACT SHEET

The Internet has become a powerful educational and communications tool, placing vast new worlds of knowledge and information in the palm of our hand. Despite its potential benefits, the Internet has been hijacked by the sex industry and allows obscenely graphic and addictive pornography to lurk only a mouse click away from innocent youth. It has also opened the door for predators and pedophiles to sexually exploit unsuspecting children. These threats adversely impact the safety, security, and quality of life for children and families with the two primary Internet dangers being the:

> **Free and easy access to all types of pornography by minor children; and,**

> **Easy and anonymous access to young children and teenagers by sexual predators.**

PROGRAM BACKGROUND: In 1998, the National Research Council (NRC) issued a congressionally mandated study and concluded that "parental education about the Internet continues to be an important part of a comprehensive program of Internet safety education for children." Furthermore, in 2000, in its report to Congress, the congressionally appointed Child Online Protection Act (COPA) Commission stated that the most effective means of protecting children from Internet content harmful to minors include: aggressive efforts toward public education; consumer empowerment efforts; law enforcement; and industry action.

As one of the nation's leading Internet safety organizations since 1994, Enough Is Enough (EIE) has continued to promote and implement its preventative approach to Internet safety, focusing on the shared responsibility between the public, the Internet industry, and the legal community. However, parents remain the 'first line of defense' in protecting their children against Internet dangers. Unfortunately, parents and other child caregivers are often overwhelmed, uninformed, or ill-equipped to deal with issues of Internet safety and need credible outside help.

EIE responded to this call-to-action in 2005 by creating the *Internet Safety 101*^{SM} program with support from the U.S. Department of Justice (OJJDP) and other partners. This state-of-the-art program addresses the critical need for parental education and empowerment. While existing Internet safety programs educate parents primarily through online methods, the comprehensive *Internet Safety 101*^{SM} program targets its resources and materials directly into the homes and hands of parents, caregivers, and educators through both traditional and online multi-media resources.

The cornerstone elements of the *Internet Safety 101*^{SM} program are the chapter-segmented DVD teaching series and corresponding workbook, which equip and empower parents, guardians, and educators to protect their homes and families from Internet dangers through a dynamic message about Internet threats and safety solutions.

The DVD series is intended to duplicate the power of in-person training seminars and features EIE President and internationally acclaimed Internet safety expert, Donna Rice Hughes. Guidelines, tips, and testimonials are also included from law enforcement/field experts, industry leaders, parents, teens, clinicians, victims of online sexual exploitation, and other leaders in the field of Internet safety.

A Special Features section includes additional 101 video packages and other helpful Internet safety resources.

The *Internet Safety 101*^{SM} training DVD series and accompanying workbook will enable individuals or groups of any size to host Internet safety training seminars geared toward parents, guardians, and educators.

Other *Internet Safety 101*^{SM} program elements include: Internet safety seminars; a train-the-trainers program; radio and print PSAs; a comprehensive list of victim resources; a *Rules 'N Tools*® resource; and online safety information at www.enough.org.

The comprehensive program educates, equips, and empowers parents, guardians, and other adult caregivers to implement Internet safety rules and software tools (*Rules 'N Tools*®) across all Internet-enabled devices and provides communities with information and resources to support local actions to increase the safety of children while online.

EIE is pleased to present a united front in the effort to promote Internet safety by partnering with key organizations dedicated to making the Internet a safer place for children and families. These partnerships include industry, government, foundation, and program distribution partners.

The Four-Part *Internet Safety 101*^{SM} DVD and workbook segments include:

ABOUT ENOUGH IS ENOUGH

INTRODUCTION
The Perfect Storm

SEGMENT 1
Pornography 101

SEGMENT 2
Predators 101

SEGMENT 3
The Evolving Internet: Web 2.0

SEGMENT 4
Safety 101

SPECIAL FEATURES

INTERNET SAFETY 101^{SM}
How to Use the DVD Series, Workbook and Rules 'N Tools® Booklet

The Internet Safety 101^{SM} DVD teaching series and accompanying workbook are the cornerstone elements of a comprehensive program to educate, equip and empower parents, educators, and other caring adults to protect children from online dangers. The Workbook and DVD can be used alone or together and have been designed for flexible, "a la carte" use.   Most of the material included is appropriate for children over the age of 16, but EIE recommends adults review the content of the DVD before showing segment elements to audiences where children are present.

Internet Safety 101^{SM} DVD

Enough Is Enough President and renowned Internet safety expert, Donna Rice Hughes, leads a live audience in this four-part DVD teaching series. The teaching series captures the power of a live seminar, without the need for a trained facilitator, by bringing the experts to you. Video Vignettes are featured throughout this comprehensive resource, which include exclusive interviews with experts from law enforcement, industry and health care, along with poignant testimonies from kids, parents, a survivor of a sexual predator, and a convicted sex offender.

The DVD can be viewed in one sitting by pressing "Play All" or in multiple sessions by viewing individual or combined chapter segments from the DVD Menu, making it ideal for individual use or groups of any size.

DVD Components

Each of the first three segments concludes with a brief Q&A exchange between Donna, subject experts, and the live audience covering helpful, non-technical safety tips, warning signs, and conversation starters.

About Enough Is Enough

Introduction: The Perfect Storm
(viewing time: 4 minutes)

Pornography 101 (Segment 1 viewing time: 36 minutes)
Every child with unrestricted Internet access is just one click away from online pornography. Learn about the risks and how to protect children from exposure.

Predators 101 (Segment 2 viewing time: 42 minutes)
Predators and pedophiles cleverly utilize the Internet to target vulnerable kids. Compelling testimonies reveal that no child is immune to the seductive tactics of a seasoned predator.

Video Vignettes (Viewing time 2 to 7 minutes each)
Each of the compelling, topical video packages featured throughout the program are also included as stand-alones, which can be used as conversation starters with friends, community members, or children. They are also an ideal tool to highlight a particular Internet concern during a community event, and can be used to promote an Internet safety event.

Web 2.0 (Segment 3 viewing time: 37 minutes)
Learn about the evolving web, the mobile Internet, social networking, online gaming and cyberbullying.

Safety 101 (Segment 4 viewing time: 19 minutes)
Safety 101 is the program "take-away". Become empowered with the essential technical and non-technical safety basics (*Rules 'N Tools®*) that can be applied across all Internet-enabled devices to protect children from the dangers discussed in the first three segments.

Special Features
Includes parental control tutorials, cyber-security resources, Ad Council PSAs, and an exclusive Interview with a convicted sex offender.

Group Use

The Internet Safety 101ᔆᔃ program's flexibility allows groups to choose a session schedule that best meets the needs of the audience.

Groups can view all four segments of the Internet Safety 101ᔆᔃ DVD (total viewing time is 2 hours and 17 minutes) in one session, individually, or in various combinations. When viewing segments in separate sessions, Enough Is Enough recommends that participants begin the first session by watching *About Enough Is Enough*, followed by *Introduction: The Perfect Storm*, and then selecting one of the first three segments.

You can choose to end each group session with the final *Safety 101* segment or wait to view the safety segment after all of the first three segments have been viewed, as depicted in the Example Format on the right.

Example Format

(Each session is approximately one hour in length, before discussion)

Session 1
- *About Enough Is Enough*
- *Introduction: The Perfect Storm*
- Segment 1: *Pornography 101*
- Discussion

Session 2
- Segment 2: *Predators 101*
- Special Features Interview: *A Convicted Sex Offender Speaks Out*
- Discussion

Session 3
- Segment 3: *Web 2.0*
- Segment 4: *Safety 101*
- Discussion

Internet Safety 101ᔆᔃ Workbook & Resource Guide

The Workbook complements, expands upon the Internet Safety DVD, and serves as a reference tool for all of the information covered in the Internet Safety DVD.

Each of the first three segments (Pornography 101, Predators 101, and Web 2.0) of the workbook includes:

- ✓ *Segment Goals:* Highlights what we will cover in each segment.
- ✓ *Follow-Along/Quick-Read Section:* Includes fill-in-the-blanks, statistics, expert's quotations, helpful tips, and summary-style information covered in the DVD, which can be used while viewing the DVD.
- ✓ *A Closer Look:* Expands upon the issues covered in each segment.
- ✓ *Warning Signs: Equips readers with vital information designed to recognize* symptoms associated with the danger addressed in the segment.
- ✓ *Empowering Parents & Rules of Engagement:* Equip readers with helpful ways to discuss Internet safety with kids.
- ✓ *Discussion Questions: Designed for a group format to encourage* conversation and application.
- ✓ *How Cyber Savvy Are You?* This end-of-segment quiz is designed to test yourself to see what you learned in each segment.
- ✓ Each segment concludes with a note-taking page for your personal use.

The fourth segment, Safety 101, expands upon the Safety Segment of the DVD and comprehensively covers the Internet safety rules and software tools Rules 'N Tools® needed to protect children on the Internet

Appendix/Resource Guide

The Appendix and Resource Guide include information about the 101 Program, the *Rules 'N Tools®* Safety Guidelines, Checklist, Parent's Pledge, Parent Buddy Check, Youth Pledge, and Age-Based Guidelines, along with a Glossary of Terms, acronyms, resource center guides, guides on tools available, including filtering, monitoring and other parental controls, video game resources, phone devices for young users, and information from our partners and sponsors.

Rules 'N Tools® Booklet

The *Rules 'N Tools®* Booklet covers the essential technical and non-technical safety basics you need to know to protect children from online dangers, including *Rules 'N Tools®* Safety Guidelines, Checklist, Parent's Pledge, Parent Buddy Check, Youth Pledge, and Age-Based Guidelines, a Glossary of Terms and acronyms to know included in Appendix A of the workbook. Enough Is Enough recommends using the *Rules 'N Tools®* Booklet in conjunction with the Internet Safety 101ᔆᔃ DVD Program.

RULES 'N TOOLS®
Internet Safety Guidelines
for Parents, Educators, and Other Caring Adults

Implement *both* safety rules and software tools to protect children online. Focus on the positives of Internet use while teaching children about the dangers and how to make wise choices online.

"RULES"

NON-TECHNICAL MEASURES

As technology continues to evolve, it is easy to feel left behind. Follow these non-technical measures to help you become a cyber-savvy, virtual parent.

❗ Establish an ongoing dialogue and keep lines of communication open:
Spend time online alongside your children and create an atmosphere of trust. Encourage your children to make good choices and temper your reactions when they run into dangers.

Teens whose parents have talked to them "a lot" about online safety are less likely to consider meeting face-to-face with someone they met on the Internet (12% vs. 20%).[i]

❗ Supervise use of all Internet-enabled devices: Keep your child's computer in an open area of your home. Monitor other points of Internet access including your child's cell phone, portable music device, gaming device, and PDA.

[i] Cox Communications Teen Internet Safety Survey, Wave II—in Partnership with the National Center for Missing & Exploited Children. March 2007. <http://www.cox.com/TakeCharge/includes/docs/survey_results_2007.ppt#271,1,Slide 1>.

❗ Know your child's online activities and friends: Be familiar with each of your children's passwords, screen names, and all account information, and have them provide the identities of every person on their buddy list or anyone they have "friended" on social networking or gaming sites. Caution your children to only communicate online with people they know in-person and who have been approved by you. Remind your children that the people they meet online may not be who they say they are.

Almost 1 in 8 teens discovered that someone they were communicating with online was an adult pretending to be much younger.[ii]

❗ Regularly check the online communities your children use, such as social networking and gaming sites, to see what information they are posting: Make sure you, as the parent, are added to your child's "friend list," because if their profiles are set to private (as they should be!), you will not be able to view any of their information. If you are unsure whether your child has a profile, conduct a simple online search through the site or by typing their name into a search engine (e.g., Google). Be aware of not only what your children are posting, but what other kids are posting about your children. Before allowing children to use social networking sites, EIE encourages parents to familiarize themselves with the content on the site and thoroughly review the safety practices and privacy tools available through that social networking site.

❗ Supervise the photos and videos your kids post and send online and through their mobile device: Photos and videos can be uploaded instantly to sites like YouTube and Facebook from any platform with Internet access including your child's cell phone, webcam, PDA, and gaming device. These images may make your child vulnerable to online predators, cyberbullies, and strangers, or lead to damaged reputations. Check with your child's school to ensure that any projects, art, or photos placed on the school website are only accessible by password (or through the school's intranet) and do not contain any personally identifiable information. Younger children should not post, text or send photos or videos.

4% of all youth Internet users in 2005 said online solicitors asked them for nude or sexually explicit photographs of themselves.[iii]

[ii] Internet Safety: Realistic Strategies & Messages for Kids Taking More and More Risks Online. Polly Klaas Foundation, 2006.

[iii] Wolak, Janis, Kimberly Mitchell, and David Finkelhor. Online Victimization of Youth: Five Years Later. Alexandria, Virginia: National Center for Missing & Exploited Children, 2006.

! **Discourage the use of webcams and mobile video devices:** Most computers, cell phones and other mobile devices now come with built-in webcam and video devices, but videos and webcams should only be used under close parental supervision or not at all. Videos should only be sent to trusted friends and family. Never allow a webcam or mobile video device to be used by your child in his or her bedroom or other private areas.

! **Teach your children how to protect personal information posted online and to follow the same rules with respect to the personal information of others:** Remind your children to **think before they post: there are no take-backs online**. Nothing is truly private on the Internet; any and all information sent or posted online is public or can be made public.

Caution your children about posting:

PERSONAL OR CONTACT INFORMATION: Your child's full name, address, phone number, passwords, and financial information should only be provided on a secure site and under parental supervision.

INTIMATE PERSONAL INFORMATION: Private, personal, and sensitive information (such as a teen's journal) should not be posted and should only be shared in private e-mails with a trusted personal friend.[iv]

REPUTATION-DAMAGING INFORMATION OR IMAGES: Inappropriate pictures (i.e., content that is explicit, suggestive, illegal, etc.), should never be posted or sent.[v]

EVENT INFORMATION: Teach children to use caution when posting information about parties, events, or activities where someone could track them down.

Teens whose parents have talked to them "a lot" about Internet safety are more concerned about the risks of sharing personal information online. For instance, 65% of teens whose parents have not talked to them about online safety post information about where they live compared to 48% of teens with more involved parents.[vi]

[iv] Willard, Nancy E. Cyber-Safe Kids, Cyber-Savvy Teens. Jossey-Bass, 2007.
[v] Ibid.
[vi] Cox Communications Teen Internet Safety Survey.

! **Be sure your children use privacy settings:** Privacy settings limit who can view your teen's profiles. On most social networking and gaming websites, your teen can change his or her privacy setting by clicking on "account settings." Ask your teens to show you the account settings or,

if you have access to your teen's account, you can check their settings for yourself. Remember that no one can detect a disguised predator, and even using these settings does not always achieve true privacy: all of your child's friends have access to and could distribute any material included on their profile.

47% of teens have an Internet profile that is public and viewable by anyone.[vii]

! Instruct your children to avoid meeting face-to-face with someone they only know online or through their mobile device: Online and mobile 'friends' may not be who they say they are. Children should be advised to come to you if anyone makes them feel scared, uncomfortable, confused, asks for any personal or personally identifiable information, or suggests meeting them.

16% of teens say they've considered meeting face-to-face with someone they've talked to only online, and 8% of teens say they have actually met in-person with someone from the Internet.[viii]

! Teach your children how to respond to cyberbullies: Children do not have to accept any online activity meant to intimidate, threaten, tease, or harm them or anyone else. Watch out for warning signs, including reluctance to go to school and reluctance to use the Internet; be aware of a change in your child's behavior and mood. Report any offensive or dangerous e-mail, chat, or other communications to local law enforcement. Do not delete the evidence. Remind your child of the Golden Rule: "Do unto others as you would have them do unto you."

Overall, 19% of teens report they have been harassed or bullied online, and the incidence of online harassment is higher (23%) among 16- and 17-year-olds. Girls are more likely to be harassed or bullied than boys (21% vs. 17%).[ix]

! Establish an agreement with your children about Internet use at home and outside of the home (see *Rules 'N Tools*® Youth Pledge): Remind them that rules for good behavior don't change just because they're on a computer. Post the agreement near the computer. Be willing to sign a parent pledge as well.

[vii] Willard, Nancy E. *Cyber-Safe Kids, Cyber-Savvy Teens.* Jossey-Bass, 2007.

[viii] Cox Communications Teen Internet Safety Survey.

[ix] Ibid.

"TOOLS"

TECHNICAL MEASURES

In addition to safety rules, protecting kids online requires the use of software tools, better known as parental controls. Parental control software helps prevent objectionable content and dangerous people from gaining access to your child. A comprehensive suite of parental control tools should include customizable filters, monitoring software, time-managing controls, and Instant Messaging (IM) and chat controls. Parental controls should be utilized on all Internet-enabled devices (desktops, laptops, and gaming, mobile, and music devices). However, these resources are not a substitute for parental supervision.

Set age-appropriate filters: Filters block categories of inappropriate websites a child can view, such as sites containing pornography, violence, gambling, and illegal drug information. Settings are password-protected. Remember that *no filter is a substitute for parental supervision,* and filters may not stop a determined child from bypassing them and accessing unsuitable content. Also, set filters to block access to peer-to-peer (P2P) networks, which allow users to connect directly to each others' computers to retrieve and swap files, without a server, and which contain tremendous amounts of pornography and child pornography.

7 out of 10 Internet users ages 8 to 18 were exposed to unwanted sexual material and more than three-quarters of unwanted exposure to pornography (79%) happened at home.[x]

Consider using monitoring software, especially if you sense your child is at risk: Monitoring software, or keystroke capture devices, can provide a full and complete record of where your child goes online, monitor outgoing and incoming communications, and identify a child's online buddies. More robust monitoring tools let parents see each website their children visit, view every e-mail or instant message they send and receive, and can even record every word they type. Many monitoring tools can send parents a periodic report summarizing their child's Internet usage and communications. These programs empower parents and guardians to set online boundaries for their children. Parents should tell their children that monitoring is being used unless the parent suspects their child is involved in risky behavior, in which case it may be better to go stealth.

[x] Generation M: Media in the Lives of 8–18 Year-olds. Henry J. Kaiser Family Foundation. 17 Nov. 2006. Wolak, Janis, Kimberly Mitchell, and David Finkelhor. Online Victimization of Youth: Five Years Later. Alexandria, Virginia: National Center for Missing & Exploited Children, 2006.

80% of sexual predators are explicit about their sexual intentions. The offenders lure teens after weeks of online conversations, playing on common teen vulnerabilities, such as their desires for romance, adventure, sexual information, and understanding. In 73% of these crimes, the youth meet the offender on multiple occasions for sexual encounters.[xi]

⚙ **Periodically check your child's online activity by viewing your browser's history:** Watch out for any sites that sound inappropriate (although not every inappropriate site has an inappropriate name!). If you notice the history has been cleared or deleted, have a discussion with your child about the sites he or she visited. Be aware that your child may selectively delete files from the history list. If you are concerned about your child's online activity, you may want to install monitoring software.

65% of all parents and 64% of all teens say that teens do things online that they wouldn't want their parents to know about.[xii]

⚙ **Set time limits:** Excessive time online, especially at night, may indicate a problem. Remind your child that Internet use is a privilege, not a right. If necessary, utilize time-limiting software tools, which allow parents to manage the amount of time and times of day their children are allowed online.

⚙ **Disallow access to chat rooms and only allow live audio chat with extreme caution:** Chat rooms are the playground of today's sexual predator; they allow immediate, direct communications between participants. Many geared toward adolescents are known for explicit sexual talk and obscene language, fostering an atmosphere which may attract online child molesters.[xiii] Chat rooms also allow users to communicate via webcam and audio chat.

Many gaming programs also come equipped with live audio chat capabilities through which individuals can alter the sound of their voice. Only mature teens should be allowed to use live audio chat. Remind your child to only interact with individuals they know offline. It's impossible for a parent, child, chat room monitor, or any technology tool to recognize a disguised, anonymous predator.

Most sexual solicitation incidents (79%) happened on home computers, beginning with personal questions about the teen's physical appearance, sexual experience, and with propositions for "cybersex."[xiv]

37% of sexual solicitation incidents happen while youth are in chat rooms, and many occur in live chat or instant-message sessions.[xv]

[xi] Finkelhor, David, Kimberly Mitchell, and Janis Wolak. National Juvenile Online Victimization Study. National Center for Missing & Exploited Children, 2007.

[xii] Lenhart, Amanda. Family, Friends & Community: Protecting Teens Online. Pew Internet & American Life Project, 2005.

[xiii] Subrahmanyam, Kaveri, David Smahel, and Patricia Greenfield. "Connecting developmental constructions to the Internet: Identity presentation and sexual exploration in online teen chat rooms." Developmental Psychology 42.3 (2006) 395-406.

⚙ **Limit your child's Instant Messaging (IM) contacts to a parent-approved buddy list:** If you decide to allow your child to use IM, block all communications from anyone not on the child's pre-approved contact list. Robust parental control software will prevent your child from adding anyone to their buddy list unless you have approved the addition. However, since some kids are able to bypass parental controls, regularly check their buddy list to ensure that it has not been altered. Be aware that many online communities, such as social networking and gaming sites, now have IM and chat features, and not all parental control software provides coverage over these new chat platforms.

⚙ **Use safe search engines:** Although search engines enable your kids to find fun websites and educational information, they can also be an efficient gateway to pornography and other objection-able content. Major search engines have addressed this need by creating child-safe zones. Some give the option of parental controls or safe searches. Consult the information on your ISP's and search engine provider's settings page to make sure that the safe search option is on.

⚙ **Set up the family's cyber-security protections:** In addition to setting up parental controls, regularly update the operating system and install a firewall and up-to-date anti-virus and anti-spyware software. The instant a computer is connected to the Internet or an "always on" broad-band connection, hackers and thieves can attempt to gain access to the family's financial and personal information. By securing your computer, you can help protect against these Internet intruders and the malicious programs that can infiltrate your computer.

⚙ **Utilize parental controls on your child's mobile phone and other mobile devices:** All of the major cell phone carriers offer parental controls of some level, including the ability to set content filters, disable or limit Internet access on Web-enabled phones. Mobile controls can also allow parents to disable, limit or monitor a child's text, picture and video messaging.

1 out of 5 teens reported that they have 'electronically sent or posted online, nude or semi-nude pictures of videos of themselves.' [xvi]

[xiv] Wolak, Janis, Kimberly Mitchell, and David Finkelhor, 2006.

[xv] Ibid.

[xiv] National Campaign to Prevent Teenage and Unplanned Pregnancy and CosmoGirl.com, 2008.

Report any content or activity that you suspect as illegal or criminal to local law enforcement and to the National Center for Missing & Exploited Children at www.cybertipline.com or at 1-800-843-5678.

ENOUGH·IS·ENOUGH
Making the Internet Safer for Children and Families

RULES 'N TOOLS® CHECKLIST
FOR PARENTS, EDUCATORS, AND OTHER CARING ADULTS

Implement *both* safety rules and software tools to protect children online. Focus on the positives of Internet use while teaching children about the dangers and how to make wise choices online.

"Rules"

☐ Establish an ongoing dialogue and keep lines of communication open.

☐ Supervise use of all Internet-enabled devices.

☐ Know your child's online activities and friends.

☐ Regularly check the online communities your children use, such as social networking and gaming sites, to see what information they are posting.

☐ Supervise the photos and videos your kids post and send online.

☐ Discourage the use of webcams and mobile video devices.

☐ Teach your children how to protect personal information posted online and to follow the same rules with respect to the personal information of others.

☐ Be sure your children use privacy settings.

☐ Instruct your children to avoid meeting face-to-face with someone they only know online or through their mobile device.

☐ Teach your children how to respond to cyberbullies.

☐ Establish an agreement with your children about Internet use at home and outside of the home
(see *Rules 'N Tools*® Youth Pledge).

"Tools"

☐ Set age-appropriate filters.

☐ Consider using monitoring software, especially if you sense your child is at risk.

☐ Periodically check your child's online activity by viewing your browser's history.

☐ Set time limits and consider using time-limiting software.

☐ Disallow access to chat rooms and only allow live audio chat with extreme caution.

☐ Limit your child's instant messaging (IM) contacts to a parent-approved buddy list.

☐ Use safe search engines.

☐ Set up the family's cyber-security protections.

☐ Utilize parental controls on your child's mobile phone and other mobile devices.

Parental controls should be utilized on all Internet-enabled devices (desktops, laptops; and gaming, mobile, and music devices). However, these resources are not a substitute for parental supervision.

Report any content or activity that you suspect as illegal or criminal to local law enforcement and to the National Center for Missing & Exploited Children at www.cybertipline.com or at 1-800-843-5678.

Rules 'N Tools®
PARENT'S PLEDGE

I pledge my commitment to implement *Rules 'N Tools®* on all Internet-enabled devices used by my children within the next _____ days.

I understand that these protective measures will help prevent objectionable content and dangerous people from gaining access to my children. Being proactive with online safety is an act of love that will help keep my children safe.

_____   _____
Parent/Guardian Signature   *Parent/Guardian Signature*

_____   _____
Date   *Date*

Rules 'N Tools®
PARENT BUDDY CHECK

The intent of the Parent Buddy Check program is to empower parents to help ensure that *Rules 'N Tools*® are implemented across all Internet-enabled devices used by their children. To provide an added safety net of support, Enough Is Enough (EIE) encourages every parent to invite another parent or a friend to be their 'Parent Buddy'. *Parents are the first line of defense!*

There are two simple steps to get the Parent Buddy Check program started:

Step 1:
Ask a buddy—a relative, friend, or a co-worker—to support your commitment to protect your children online as represented by your *Rules 'N Tools*® Parent's Pledge.

_____   _____
Buddy Signature   *Date*

_____
E-mail Address

Step 2:
To promote greater awareness throughout your community, talk regularly with your 'Parent Buddy' and with your friends about the importance of Internet Safety, and be sure to check EIE's website at www.enough.org for the latest tools and resources to protect your family on the Internet.

Together we can make a difference for the sake of the children!

Rules 'N Tools®
YOUTH PLEDGE

I have spoken with my parent/guardian about the following and am aware that:

☐ Nothing is truly private, and there are "no take-backs" online and through my mobile device.

☐ Some people online may try to befriend me who want to harm me.

☐ It is not my fault if I see something bad accidentally.

☐ Private family matters should not be discussed online or via text. Instead, I should talk about them with a parent or other trusted adult.

☐ My parents may supervise my time online and may use a filtering and/or monitoring service. This is because they are concerned about my safety.

☐ Internet use and mobile access is a privilege, not a right. I will follow the guidelines of my *Rules 'N Tools®* Youth Pledge whenever I have access to the Internet, both in and out of my home or through my mobile device.

I agree to:

☐ Talk with my parents to learn the rules for using the Internet, including where I can go, what I can do, when I can go online, and how long I can be online (_____ minutes or _____ hours).

☐ Always tell my parents immediately if I see or receive anything on the Internet, my phone or other mobile device that makes me feel uncomfortable or threatened, including e-mail messages, websites, images, chats, or even anything in the regular mail from Internet friends.

☐ Protect my personal information, such as my home address, telephone number, my parents' names, work addresses or telephone numbers, credit card numbers, or the name and location of my school or any club or team. I will talk to my parents before giving out this information. I will keep this rule when I am communicating via chat rooms, instant message (IM), e-mail, websites, online games, text messaging, or social networking sites, and when entering contests and registering for online clubs.

☐ Check with my parents before posting or sending pictures or videos of myself, other family members, or other people through the Internet, text or regular mail.

☐ Never give out my Internet passwords to anyone (even my best friends) other than my parents.

☐ Treat others online as I would have them treat me. I will never send threatening or mean messages, nor will I respond to any such messages that are sent to me. I will not do anything online that could hurt or anger others or do anything that is against the law.

☐ Never download, install, or copy any copyright information from the Internet without proper permission from the site and my parents.

☐ Never do anything on the Internet or on my cell phone or other mobile device that costs money without first asking permission from my parents.

☐ Only fill out any online forms or questionnaires with the permission of my parents.

☐ Never open or accept e-mails, enclosures, links, URLs, texts, videos or pictures or other information from people I do not know.

☐ Never tell anyone online where I will be or what I will be doing without permission from my parents.

☐ Never enter a chat room unless given prior permission from my parents.

☐ Avoid in-person meetings with anyone I met or befriended online or through my mobile device without parental permission and being accompanied by a parent. I know that not everyone I meet online is who they say they are, and I cannot detect a disguised predator.

☐ Follow my family's Internet safety guidelines when accessing the Internet through an Internet-enabled device, while at a friend's house, and also when at school.

☐ Only instant message (IM) people on my buddy list who have been previously approved by my parents.

☐ Log off or turn off my computer if I come across something bad online. I will then tell my parents what happened as soon as possible.

☐ Make my parents aware of **all** of my Internet logon, chat names, gamertags, and social networking pro-file names listed below:

_____

_____

_____

_____   _____
Youth's Signature   Parent's Signature

_____   _____
Date   Date

Parents may use this pledge for their children, tailor this pledge to meet the specific needs of their family, or work with their children to create a youth pledge together!

Rules 'N Tools®
AGE-BASED GUIDELINES

Remember to use Enough Is Enough's Internet Safety *Rules 'N Tools®* to protect your kids at every age!

Key principles for all age groups include to:

⊙ Keep lines of communication open.

⊙ Create a list of Internet rules with your kids (see *Rules 'N Tools®* Youth Pledge).

⊙ Set parental controls at the age-appropriate levels and use filtering and monitoring tools as a complement—not a replacement—for parental supervision.

⊙ Supervise all Internet-enabled devices and keep computers in a public area of the house.

⊙ Talk to your kids about healthy sexuality in the event they come across sexually explicit, online pornography at home, school, a friend's house, or the library.

⊙ Encourage your kids to come to you if they encounter anything online that makes them feel uncomfortable or threatened. (Stay calm and don't blame the child; otherwise, they won't turn to you for help when they need it.)

⊙ Teach them not to interact with people they don't know offline because an online predator can easily disguise him/herself.

⊙ Check the history file on your computer to see which sites your child has accessed.

TWO- TO FOUR-YEAR-OLDS

KIDS AT THIS AGE:	GUIDELINES:
⊙ Will accept media content at face value	⊙ Always sit with your child at the computer (EIE recommends that children at this age not be exposed to the Internet).
⊙ Don't have the critical thinking skills to be online alone	⊙ Parents can begin teaching basic computer skills by introducing age-appropriate games and educational programs.
⊙ May be frightened by media images, both real and fictional	
⊙ Risk moving from appropriate to inappropriate sites through hyperlinks	

FIVE- TO SEVEN-YEAR-OLDS

KIDS AT THIS AGE:	GUIDELINES:
⊙ Are very capable at using computers and cell phones (i.e., following commands, using the mouse, and playing computer games)	Always sit with your children when they are online.
⊙ Will accept media content at face value	⊙ If children are introduced to the Internet, parents are encouraged to:
⊙ Don't have the critical thinking skills to be online or text alone	1. Use kid-friendly search engines and/or "walled gardens" with parental controls. *(See Appendix B-8 for a list of kid-friendly search engines.)*
⊙ May be frightened by media images, both real and fictional	2. Set age-appropriate filtering at the most restrictive level.
⊙ May be unintentionally exposed to inappropriate websites	3. Create a personalized online environment by limiting your kids to their list of favorite or "bookmarked" sites.
⊙ Are vulnerable to online marketers who encourage them to give out personal information through surveys, contests, and registration forms	4. Keep Internet-connected computers in an open area where you can easily monitor your kids' activities.
⊙ Risk moving from appropriate to inappropriate sites through hyperlinks	5. Start teaching kids about privacy. Tell them never to give out information about themselves or their family when online.
	6. Have your kids use an online nickname if a site encourages them to submit their names to "personalize" the web content.
	7. Block or disallow the use of instant messaging (IM), e-mail, chat rooms, mobile Internet, text , picture and video messaging, and access to or message boards at this age.

NOTE: Services such as The Children's Internet offer children safe, age-appropriate Internet experience available for a monthly fee. If you do allow your child to use a mobile device, use a kid-friendly mobile device (See B-16).

EIGHT- TO TEN-YEAR-OLDS

KIDS AT THIS AGE:

- Are interested in the activities of older kids in their lives, are starting to develop a sense of their own identity, and they tend to be trusting and do not often question authority

- Enjoy surfing online and using mobile devices for fun and playing interactive games

- May be using e-mail and may also experiment with instant messaging (IM), chat rooms, and message boards (online forums), social networking and other interactive sites, and mobile devices although the use of these programs is strongly discouraged at this age

- Are curious and interested in discovering new information

- Lack the critical thinking skills to be online alone

- Are vulnerable to online marketers who encourage them to give out personal information through surveys, contests, and registration forms

- May be frightened by realistic portrayals of violence, threats, or dangers

- May begin to communicate with online acquaintances they may not know in real life

- May be influenced by media images and personalities, especially those that appear "cool" or desirable

- May be exposed to search results with links to inappropriate websites

- Are vulnerable to online predators if they use chat rooms, message boards, social networking, text messaging or instant messaging (IM)

GUIDELINES:

- Sit with your kids when they are online, or make sure they only visit sites you have approved.

- Keep any Internet-connected computer in an open area where you can closely monitor your child's online use.

- Set parental controls at the age-appropriate levels and use filtering and monitoring tools as a complement—not a replacement—for parental supervision.

- Use kid-friendly search engines or search engines with parental controls.

- Do not allow instant messaging, chat rooms, or social networking sites intended for older audiences at this age. *(See Appendix B-12 for a list of social networking sites for younger children.)*

- You and your child should have the same e-mail address. Establish a shared family e-mail account with your Internet service provider rather than letting your kids have their own accounts.

- Get to know your child's online activities and friends. Talk to your kids about their online friends and activities just as you would about their other activities.

- Teach your kids to always come to you before giving out information through e-mail, message boards, registration forms, personal profiles, and online contests.

ELEVEN- TO THIRTEEN-YEAR-OLDS

KIDS AT THIS AGE:

- Can be highly influenced by what their friends are doing online and crave more independence

- Tend to use the Internet to help with school work, to download music, e-mail others, play online games, and go to sites of interest

- Enjoy communicating with friends by instant messaging (IM) and chat features, and text messaging on their cell phones

- Lack the critical thinking skills to judge the accuracy of online information

- Feel in control when it comes to technology

- Are vulnerable to online marketers who encourage them to give out personal information through surveys, contests, and registration forms

- Are at a sensitive time in their sexual development—particularly boys—and may look for pornographic sites. Girls may try to imitate provocative media images and behaviors.

- Are interested in building relationships (especially girls) with online acquaintances, and are susceptible to crushes on older teens or young adults

- Are at the most vulnerable age range to become victims of sexual predators

- May be bullied or may be bullying others online

GUIDELINES:

- Keep Internet-connected computers in an open area and out of your children's bedrooms.

- Set parental controls at the age-appropriate levels and use filtering and monitoring tools as a complement—not a replacement—for parental supervision. Use parental controls on all Internet-enabled devices such as cell phones, gaming devices, iPods, and PDAs.

- Talk with your kids about their online friends and activities just as you would about their offline activities.

- Instruct your child to avoid face-to-face meetings with anyone they only know online. "Online friends" may not be who they claim to be.

- Teach your kids never to give out personal information without your permission when participating in online activities (including e-mail, chat rooms or instant messaging, filling out registration forms and personal profiles, and entering online contests).

- Insist on access and passwords to your kids' e-mail and instant messaging accounts to make sure that they're not talking to strangers. Limit instant messaging to a parent-approved buddy list.

- Talk to your kids about ethical online behavior. They should not be using the Internet to spread gossip, bully, or make threats against others.

- Disallow chat rooms.

- Do periodic spot checks (like checking browser history files) to monitor your kids' online behaviors.

- Limit time online.

- Do not allow your children to have online profiles or pages on social networking sites that have a minimum age requirement such as MySpace (thirteen years old) and Facebook (thirteen years old). (Kids can lie about their ages and gain access to these sites.) Only allow your children to access YouTube with caution. Sites such as Imbee, ClubPenguin, and TweenLand are more appropriate for users under fourteen years of age. Follow the *Rules 'N Tools®* Parent's Guideline regarding social networking sites.

- Your children should not post pictures or videos unless under close parental supervision.

FOURTEEN- TO EIGHTEEN-YEAR-OLDS

KIDS AT THIS AGE:

⊙ Crave both group identity and independence

⊙ Tend to download music, use instant messaging (IM), e-mail, social networking sites, and play online games; most of them have visited chat rooms, and many have participated in adult or private chat

⊙ May push the boundaries of safe online behavior by looking for gross humor, gore, gambling, or explicit adult sites

⊙ Are more critical and selective in their media interests and activities

⊙ Are more likely to receive unwanted sexual comments online

⊙ Receive the highest percentage of pornographic spam

⊙ Are interested in building relationships with online acquaintances (especially true of girls)

⊙ Are more likely to be asked for a real-life meeting by an online acquaintance, and more apt to accept

⊙ Are still vulnerable to online marketers who encourage them to give out personal information through surveys, contests, and registration forms

⊙ May be bullied or be bullying others online

⊙ Are more likely to use credit cards online

⊙ May be experimenting with online gambling

REMEMBER: A teen's prefrontal cortex is not fully developed at this age; teens still need your guidance!

GUIDELINES:

⊙ Create a list of Internet house rules with your teens (see *Rules 'N Tools®* Youth Pledge). You should include the kinds of sites that are off limit.

⊙ Set parental controls at the age-appropriate levels and use filtering and monitoring tools as a complement—not a replacement—for parental supervision. Use parental controls on all Internet-enabled devices such as cell phones, gaming devices, iPods, and PDAs.

⊙ Keep Internet-connected computers in an open area and out of your teens' bedrooms.

⊙ Talk to them about their online friends and activities just as you would about their offline activities.

⊙ Talk to your teens about their IM list and make sure they're not talking to strangers. Your teens should only use parent-approved buddy lists and you should check their lists regularly to make sure your teens do not alter them.

⊙ Insist that your teens tell you first if they want to meet an "online friend." Then check out the online friend, and if you feel the online friend is safe, accompany your child to the meeting.

⊙ Teach your teens to protect personal information (see *Rules 'N Tools®*).

⊙ Help protect them from spam. Tell your teens not to give out their e-mail address online or respond to junk mail, and to use e-mail filters.

⊙ Teach your teens responsible online behavior. File-sharing and taking text, images, or artwork from the web may infringe on copyright laws.

⊙ Talk to them about ethical behavior. They should not be using the Internet to spread gossip, bully, or threaten others.

⊙ Oversee financial transactions online, including ordering, buying, or selling items.

⊙ Discuss gambling and its potential risks, and remind your teens that it is illegal for them to gamble online.

⊙ Do periodic spot checks (like checking browser history files) to monitor your kids' online behaviors.

REMEMBER: Kids are safest if not on social networking sites. Follow the *Rules 'N Tools®* if you allow your teens to use them.

Internet Safety 101℠
GLOSSARY OF TERMS

Adware: A form of malicious code that displays unsolicited advertising on your computer.

Anti-virus Software: Software that attempts to block malicious programs/code/software (called viruses or malware) from harming your computer.

Blog/Blogging (short for web log): A diary or personal journal kept on a website. Blogs are usually updated frequently and sometimes entries are grouped by specific subjects, such as politics, news, pop culture, or computers. Readers often post comments in response to blog entries.

Bookmark: A saved link to a website that has been added to a list of saved links or favorite sites (i.e., "Favorites") that you can click on directly, rather than having to retype the address when revisiting the site.

Browser: A program that lets you find, see, and hear material on web pages. Popular browsers include Netscape Navigator, Safari, Microsoft Internet Explorer, Firefox, and Chrome.

Buddies (Buddy List): A list of friends a user interacts with online through various media such as instant messaging (IM) and chat.

CDA: The Communications Decency Act of 1996, a part of the Telecommunications Act of 1996, was the first attempt by the U.S. Congress to protect children on the Internet from pornography. CDA prohibited knowingly sending or displaying "indecent" material to minors through the computer, defined as: "any comment, request, suggestion, proposal, image, or other communication that, in context, depicts or describes, in terms of patently offensive as measured by contemporary community standards, sexual or excretory activities or organs." The Act was immediately challenged by a law suit by the ACLU and blocked by a lower court. A year later the U.S. Supreme Court struck down the indecency provisions of the CDA in the historical cyberlaw case of *Reno v. ACLU* (1997). The Supreme Court held that a law that places a "burden on adult speech is unacceptable if less restrictive alternatives would be at least as effective in achieving" the same goal.[xvi] However, the court reaffirmed the application of obscenity and child pornography laws in cyberspace—an important victory for the protection of children online.

Chat Room: A location online that allows multiple users to communicate electronically with each other in real time, as opposed to delayed time as with e-mail.

[xvi] *Reno v. ACLU*, 521 U.S. 844 (1997).

Circumventor Sites: Parallel websites that allow children to get around filtering software and access sites that have been blocked.

Closed Systems: A limited network of sites that are rated and categorized by maturity level and quality. Within a closed system, children cannot go beyond the network white list of approved websites, also referred to as a "walled garden."

Cookie: A piece of information about your visit to a website that some websites record automatically on your computer. By using a cookie, a website operator can determine a lot of information about you and your computer. Cookies are not always bad. For example, a cookie remembers that you prefer aisle seats in the front of the plane.

COPA: The Child Online Protection Act (COPA) of 1998 was an effort by the U.S. Congress to modify the CDA in response to the Supreme Court's decision in *Reno v. ACLU*. The law sought to make it a crime for commercial websites to make pornographic material that is "harmful to minors" available to juveniles. The purpose of COPA was to protect children from instant access to pornographic "teaser images" on porn syndicate web pages, by requiring pornographers to take credit card numbers, adult verification numbers, or access codes to restrict children's access to pornographic material and to allow access to this material

for consenting adults only. Despite the critical need for measures to protect children from accessing harmful materials, the law was immediately challenged and blocked by lower courts, and has become the subject of an epic legal battle, still raging today. The permanent injunction against the enforcement of COPA remains in effect today. The government has not announced whether it will appeal the case to the U.S. Supreme Court for a third time.

COPPA: The Children's Online Privacy Protection Act of 1998, which went into effect in April 2000, requires websites that market to children under the age of 13 to get "verifiable parental consent" before allowing children access to their sites.[xvii] The Federal Trade Commission (FTC), which is responsible for enforcing COPPA, adopted a sliding scale approach to obtaining parental consent.[xviii] The sliding scale approach allows website operators to use a mix of methods to comply with the law, including print-and-fax forms, follow-up phone calls and e-mails, and credit card authorizations.

CIPA: The Children's Internet Protection Act (CIPA) of 2000 requires public schools and libraries receiving federal e-rate funds to use a portion of those funds to filter their Internet access. They must filter out obscenity on library computer terminals used by adults and both obscenity and harmful-to-minors materials on terminals used by minor children. CIPA was upheld by the U.S. Supreme Court as constitutional in June 2003.

[xvii] <www.coppa.org/coppa.htm>.

[xviii] See: Federal Trade Commission, How to Comply with The Children's Online Privacy Protection Rule, November 1999. <www.ftc.gov/bcp/online/pubs/buspubs/coppa.htm>.

Cyberbullies/Cyberbullying: Willful and repeated harm inflicted through the medium of electronic text, typically through e-mails or on websites (e.g., blogs, social networking sites).

Cybercrime: Any Internet-related illegal activity.

Cybersecurity: Any technique, software, etc., used to protect computers and prevent online crime.

Cybersex (computer sex, or "cybering"): Refers to virtual sexual encounters between two or more persons.

Cyberstalking: Methods individuals use to track, lure, or harass another person online.

Discussion Boards: Also called Internet forums, message boards, and bulletin boards. These are online sites that allow users to post comments on a particular issue.

Domain Name: The part of an Internet address to the right of the final dot used to identify the type of organization using the server, such as .gov or .com.

Download: To copy a file from one computer system to another via the Internet (usually your computer or mobile device).

Electronic Footprint: Computers maintain a record of all website visits and e-mail messages, leaving a trail of the user's activity in cyberspace. These data can still exist even after the browser history has been cleared and e-mail messages have been deleted.

Electronic Mail (E-Mail): An electronic mail message sent from one computer or mobile device to another computer or mobile device.

Favorite(s): The name for bookmarks (see above) used by Microsoft's Internet Explorer browser.

File Sharing: This software enables multiple users to access the same computer file simultaneously. File sharing sometimes is used illegally to download music or software.

Filter/Filtering: Allows you to block certain types of content from being displayed. Some of the things you can screen for include course language, nudity, sexual content, and violence. Different methods to screen unwanted Internet content include whitelisting, blacklisting, monitoring activity, keyword recognition, or blocking-specific functions such as e-mail or instant messages (IM). Filtering options are available through parental control software.

Firewall: A security system usually made up of hardware and software used to block hackers, viruses, and other malicious threats to your computer.

Flame: A hostile, strongly worded message that may contain obscene language.

Gamer Tag: The nickname a user has chosen to be identified by when playing Internet games.

Gaming: Internet games, which can be played either individually or by multiple online users at the same time.

Griefers: Internet gamers who intentionally cause problems and/or cyberbully other gamers (i.e., individuals who play online games).

Grooming: Refers to the techniques sexual predators use to get to know and seduce their victims in preparation for sexual abuse.

Hardware: A term for the actual computer equipment and related machines or computer parts.

History: A tracking feature of Internet browsers that shows all the recent websites visited.

Homepage: The site that is the starting point on the web for a particular group or organization.

Identity Theft: In this crime, someone obtains the vital information (e.g., credit card, Social Security Number, bank account numbers) of another person, usually to steal money. E-mail scams, spyware, and viruses are among the most typical methods for stealing someone's identity.

Instant Message/Messaging (IM): Private, real-time text conversation between two users.

Internet (Net): A giant collection of computer networks that connects people and information all over the world.

Internet Relay Chat (IRC): A multi-use live chat facility. IRC is an area of the Internet comprising thousands of chat rooms. IRC is run by IRC servers and requires client software to use.

Internet Service Provider (ISP): A generic term for any company that can connect you directly to the Internet.

JPEG (Joint Partner Experts Group or Joint Photographic Experts Group): A popular file format for graphic images on the Internet.

Malware: Stands for malicious software or code, which includes any harmful code—trojans, worms, spyware, adware, etc.—that is designed to damage the computer or collect information.

Mobile Web: The World Wide Web as accessed from mobile devices such as cell phones, PDAs, and other portable gadgets connected to a public network. Access does not require a desktop computer.

Modem: A device installed in your computer or an external piece of hardware that connects your computer to the Internet through a phone or cable line and allows communication between computers.

Monitoring Software: Software products that allow parents to monitor or track the websites or e-mail messages that a child visits or reads.

Mouse: A small hand-controlled device for pointing and clicking to make selections on the screen.

Netiquette: Rules or manners for interacting courteously with others online (such as not typing a message in all capital letters, which is equivalent to shouting).

Password: A secret word or number that must be used to gain access to an online service or to modify software, such as a parental control.

Parental Controls: Specific features or software that allow parents to manage the online activities of children.

Peer-to-Peer (P2P) Computing: A method of sharing files directly over the Internet from one Internet-enabled device to another (computer, mobile phone, etc.), without being routed through a server.

Phishing: A scam that involves sending a fraudulent e-mail soliciting credit card, Social Security, or other personal information from an unsuspecting user.

Post: To upload information to the web.

Real Time: "Live" time; the actual time during which something takes place.

Search Engine: An Internet service that helps you search for information on the web.

Sexting: Cell phone, computer and other mobile device users—often teens and 'tweens'—create and exchange provocative messages and nude, sexual images of themselves using their cell phone's built-in digital camera and text messaging capabilities.

Skype™: A popular computer program that enables users to set up profiles, make free phone calls, chat, and video chat through their computer or mobile device from any point around the world. This free service functions through a "peer-to-peer" network, which allows individuals to communicate directly with each other rather than through a central server. Since the conversations and content exchanged through Skype are not scrutinized by monitors, children are at risk of exposure to inappropriate material and dangerous people.

SMS: Stands for "Short Message Service," a form of text messaging on cell phones, sometimes used between computers and cell phones.

Social Networks: Online communities where people share information about themselves, music files, photos, etc. There are many social networking websites (e.g., MySpace, Facebook, or Friendster).

Software: A program, or set of instructions, that runs on a computer.

Spam: Any unsolicited e-mail, or junk mail. Most spam is either a money scam or sexual in nature. Internet Service Providers, e-mail software, and other software can help block some, but not all, spam.

Spyware: A wide variety of software installed on people's computers, which collects information about you without your knowledge or consent and sends it back to whoever wrote the spyware program. The programs typically will track computer use and create numerous pop-up ads. In some instances, the spyware can damage the computer and facilitate *identity theft*.

Surfing: Similar to channel surfing on a television, Internet surfing involves users browsing around various websites following whatever interests them.

Texting: A method of sending short messages (also called SMSes, txts, or text messaging) between mobile phones and other computer-enabled devices.

Twitter: Twitter is a social media site that lets its users send short messages (or "tweets") to a network of connected users online. Twitter is similar in form to features on other social networking and instant messaging sites that allow users to update their "status" or leave an "away message" to let their friends know what they are up to in real-time, all the time. On Twitter, this is also called "micro-blogging"; individuals have 140 characters to let the world know what's on their mind or to send a tweet about something they care about.

Uniform Resource Locator (URL): The address of a site on the Internet. For example, the URL for the White House is: www.whitehouse.gov. Each URL is unique and there are millions of them.

Upload: To send information from your computer to another computer.

Username: The name a user selects to be identified on a computer, on a network, or in an online gaming forum.

Videocam (Webcam): Video cameras that are often attached to a computer so that a video image can be sent to another while communicating online.

Virus: A self-replicating software program that typically arrives through e-mail attachments and which multiplies on the hard drive, quickly exhausting the computer's memory. A trojan is a variation that allows unauthorized users access to the computer, from which they can send infected e-mails or spam.

Wireless Computers: Many networks now allow computers access to the Internet without being connected with wires. These networks are becoming increasingly more popular and powerful, allowing people to access the Internet using cell phones and other devices.

World Wide Web (WWW or Web): A hypertext-based navigation system on the Internet that lets you browse through a variety of linked resources, using typed commands or clicking on hot links.

ENOUGH·IS·ENOUGH
Making the Internet Safer for Children and Families

Internet Safety 101℠

TOP 50 INTERNET ACRONYMS
PARENTS *NEED* TO KNOW

1. **8:** it refers to oral sex

2. **1337:** it means elite

3. **143:** it means I love you

4. **182:** it means I hate you

5. **459:** it also means I love you

6. **1174:** it means nude club

7. **420:** it refers to marijuana

8. **ADR or addy:** Address

9. **ASL:** Age/Sex/Location

10. **banana:** it means penis

11. **CD9:** it means Code 9 = parents are around

12. **DUM:** Do You Masturbate?

13. **DUSL:** Do You Scream Loud?

14. **FB:** F*** Buddy

15. **FMLTWIA:** F*** Me Like The Whore I Am

16. **FOL:** Fond Of Leather

17. **GNOC:** Get Naked On Cam (webcam)

18. **GYPO:** Get Your Pants Off

19. **IAYM:** I Am Your Master

20. **IF/IB:** In the Front or In the Back

21. **IIT:** Is It Tight?

22. **ILF/MD:** I Love Female/Male Dominance

23. **IMEZRU:** I Am Easy, Are You?

24. **IWSN:** I Want Sex Now

25. **J/O:** Jerking Off

26. **KFY:** Kiss For You

27. **kitty:** it means vagina

28. **KPC:** Keeping Parents Clueless

29. **LMIRL:** Let's Meet In Real Life

30. **MOOS:** Member(s) Of the Opposite Sex

31. **MOSS or MOTSS:** Member(s) Of The Same Sex

32. **MorF:** Male or Female

33. **MOS:** Mom Over Shoulder

34. **MPFB:** My Personal F*** Buddy

35. **NALOPKT:** Not A Lot Of People Know That

36. **NIFOC:** Nude In Front Of Computer

37. **NMU:** Not Much, You?

38. **P911:** Parent Alert

39. **PAL:** Parents Are Listening

40. **PAW:** Parents Are Watching

41. **PIR:** Parent In Room

42. **POS:** Parent Over Shoulder

43. **PRON:** Porn

44. **Q2C:** Quick To Cum

45. **RU/18:** Are You Over 18?

46. **RUH:** Are You Horny?

47. **S2R:** Send To Receive (pictures)

48. **SorG:** Straight or Gay

49. **TDTM:** Talk Dirty To Me

50. **WYCM:** Will You Call Me?

Be sure to sign up for the **E-mail Word of the Day:**

www.netlingo.com/subscribe.php

Internet Safety 101℠
RESOURCE GUIDE *(ABBREVIATED)*

Enough Is Enough's (EIE's) website houses a comprehensive list of other Internet safety resources, along with an extensive list of secular and faith-based victim resources for those searching for healing from the harms of pornography, sexual addiction, and sexual abuse. Visit The Resources Center at www.enough.org.

PARENTS, GUARDIANS & EDUCATORS

American Family Association

P.O. Drawer 2440
Tupelo, MS 38803

PHONE: 1-662-844-5036

www.afa.net

Center for Children and Technology

96 Morton Street, 7th Floor
New York, NY 10014

PHONE: 1-212-807-4200
FAX: 1-212-633-8804

http://cctedc.org

Center for Safe and Responsible Internet Use (CSRIU)

474 W. 29th Avenue
Eugene, OR 97405

PHONE: 1-541-344-9125
FAX: 1-541-344-1481
E-MAIL: contact@csriu.org

www.csriu.org

Childnet International

Studio 14
Brockley Cross Business Centre
96 Endwell Road
London, SE4 2PD

PHONE: +44 (0)20 7639 6967
FAX: +44 (0)20 7639 7027
E-MAIL: info@childnet.com

www.childnet-int.org

Child Quest International, Inc.

1060 N. 4th Street
Suite 200
San Jose, CA 95112

PHONE: 1-408-287-4673 (HOPE)
FAX: 1-408-287-4676
E-MAIL: info@childquest.org

www.childquest.org

Children's Defense Fund

25 E Street NW
Washington, DC 20001

TOLL FREE: 1-800-CDF-1200
          (1-800-233-1200)
PHONE: 1-202-628-8787
E-MAIL: cdfinfo@
childrensdefense.org

www.childrensdefense.org

The Children's Partnership

1351 3rd Street Promenade
Suite 206
Santa Monica, CA 90401

PHONE: 1-310-260-1220
FAX: 1-310-260-1921
E-MAIL: frontdoor@
childrenspartnership.org

www.childrenspartnership.org

Citizens for Community Values

11175 Reading Road, #103
Cincinnati, OH 45241

PHONE: 1-513-733-5775

www.ccv.org

Concerned Women for America

1015 Fifteenth Street, NW
Suite 1100
Washington DC 20005

PHONE: 1-202-488-7000
FAX: 1-202-488-0806

www.cwfa.org

Congressional Internet Caucus

CONTACT: Allison Rodway
PHONE: 1-202-638-4370
E-MAIL: arodway@netcaucus.org

www.netcaucus.org

ConnectSafely

www.connectsafely.org

Cyberangels

P.O. Box 3171
Allentown, PA 18106

PHONE: 1-610-351-8250
FAX: 1-610-482-9101

www.cyberangels.org

Darkness to Light

7 Radcliffe Street
Suite 200
Charleston, SC 29403

PHONE: 1-843-965-5444
FAX: 1-843-965-5449

www.darkness2light.org

ECPAT – USA
End Child Prostitution, Child Pornography and Trafficking of Children for Sexual Purposes

157 Montague Street
Brooklyn, NY 11201

PHONE: 1-718-935-9192
FAX: 1-718-935-9173

www.ecpatusa.org

Enough Is Enough

746 Walker Road, Suite 116
Great Falls, VA 22066

TOLL FREE: 1-888-744-0004
PHONE: 1-703-476-7890

www.enough.org

Family Online Safety Institute (FOSI)

815 Connecticut Avenue
Suite 220
Washington, DC 20006

PHONE: 1-202-572-6252
E-MAIL: moconnor@dcgpr.com

www.fosi.org

Family Research Council

801 G Street NW
Washington, DC 20001

TOLL FREE: 1-800-225-4008
PHONE: 1-202-393-2100

www.frc.org

Focus on the Family

8605 Explorer Drive
Colorado Springs, CO 80920

TOLL FREE: 1-800-A-Family
(1-800-232-6459)

www.family.org

Free The Slaves

514 10th Street, NW, 7th Floor
Washington, DC 20004

PHONE: 1-202-638-1865
E-MAIL: info@freetheslaves.net

www.freetheslaves.net

GetNetWise

Internet Education Foundation
1634 Eye Street NW
Washington DC 2009

PHONE: 1-202-638-4370
E-MAIL: webmaster@getnetwise.org

www.getnetwise.com

iKeepSafe

Internet Keep Safe Coalition℠ Headquarters
4607 N. 40th St.
Arlington, VA 22207

TOLL FREE: 1-866-794-7233
PHONE: 1-703-536-1637
FAX: 1-703-852-7100
E-MAIL: info@iKeepSafe.org

www.ikeepsafe.org

International Justice Mission

P.O. Box 58147
Washington, DC 20037

PHONE: 1-703-465-5495
FAX: 1-703-465-5499

www.ijm.org

i-SAFE Inc.

5900 Pasteur Court
Suite 100
Carlsbad, CA 92008

PHONE: 1-760-603-7911
FAX: 1-760-603-8382

www.isafe.org

Look Both Ways

www.ilookbothways.com

Morality in the Media

475 Riverside Drive, Suite 239
New York, NY 10115

PHONE: 1-212-870-3222
FAX: 1-212-870-2765

EMAIL: mim@moralityinmedia.org

www.moralityinmedia.org

MySpace, MyKids

660 Preston Forest Center
Dallas, TX 75230

PHONE: 1-214-580-2003
E-MAIL: info@myspacemykids.com

www.myspacemykids.com

MySpace Safety Tips for Parents

www.myspace.com

The National Center for Missing and Exploited Children

Charles B. Wang International Children's Building

699 Prince Street
Alexandria, Virginia 22314-3175

TOLL FREE: 1-888-246-2632
PHONE: 1-703-274-3900
FAX: 1-703-274-2200
24-HOUR HOTLINE: 1-800-THE-LOST
            (1-800-843-5678)

www.missingkids.com

National Coalition for the Protection of Children and Families

800 Compton Road, Suite 9224
Cincinnati, OH 45231

PHONE: 1-513-521-6227

www.nationalcoalition.org

National Committee to Prevent Child Abuse

Tennyson Center for Children at Colorado Christian Home

2950 Tennyson Street
Denver, CO 80212

TOLL FREE: 1-877-224-8223
PHONE: 1-303-433-2541
FAX: 1-303-433-9701

www.childabuse.org

National Law Center for Children and Families

225 North Fairfax Street
Alexandria, VA 22314

PHONE: 1-703-548-5522
FAX: 1-703-548-5544

www.nationallawcenter.org

National Parent Teacher Association

National Headquarters

541 N. Fairbanks Court
Suite 1300
Chicago, IL 60611-3396

TOLL FREE: 1-800-307-4PTA (4782)
PHONE: 1-312-670-6782
FAX: 1-312-670-6783
E-MAIL: info@pta.org

www.pta.org

National Parent Teacher Association/Office of Programs and Public Policy

1400 L Street, NW
Suite 300
Washington, DC 20005-9998

PHONE: 1-202-289-6790
FAX: 1-202-289-6791

National School Boards Association

1680 Duke Street
Alexandria, VA 22314

PHONE: 1-703-838-6722
FAX: 1-703-683-7590

www.nsba.org

The National Urban League

120 Wall Street
New York, NY 10005

PHONE: 1-212-558-5300
FAX: 1-212-344-5332

www.nul.org

Net Family News

www.NetFamilyNews.org

NetSmartz411

CONTACT: Hotline Staff
PHONE: 1-888-NETS411
        1-888-638-7411

www.netsmartz411.org

Plan 2 Succeed

641 Shunpike Rd #123
Chatham, NJ 07928

E-MAIL: info@plan2succeed.org

www.plan2succeed.org

Polaris Project

P.O. Box 77892
Washington, DC 20013

PHONE: 1-202-745-1001
FAX: 1-202-745-1119
E-MAIL: DC@polarisproject.org

www.polarisproject.org

Project Online Safety

www.projectonlinesafety.com

Protect Kids

www.protectkids.com

Rape, Abuse & Incest National Network (RAINN)

2000 L Street, NW
Suite 406
Washington, DC 20036

PHONE: 1-202-544-3064
FAX: 1-202-544-3556
E-MAIL: info@rainn.org

www.rainn.org

SafeSurf

www.safesurf.com

Sexual Abuse Free Environment (S.A.F.E.)

E-MAIL: publisher@
thosearemyprivateparts.com

www.thosearemyprivateparts.com
www.safeincorporated.com

Staysafe

E-MAIL: contact@staysafe.org

www.staysafe.org

Stop Internet Predators

1919 M Street, NW
Suite 470
Washington, DC 20036

PHONE: 1-202-416-0257
FAX: 1-202-416-0256
E-MAIL:
info@stopinternetpredators.org

www.stopinternetpredators.org

TechMission

31 Torrey Street, Unit 1
Boston, MA 02124

PHONE: 1-617-282-9798
FAX: 1-617-825-0313

www.techmission.org

Web Wise Kids

P.O. Box 27203
Santa Ana, CA 92799

TOLL FREE: 1-866-WEB-WISE
PHONE: 1-714-435-2885
FAX: 1-714-435-0523
E-MAIL: infor@webwisekids.org

www.webwisekids.org

Wired Safety

One Bridge Street
Irvington-on-Hudson, NY 10533

PHONE: 1-201-463-8663
FAX: 1-201-670-7002
E-MAIL: parry@aftab.com

ASSOCIATED SITES:
www.KatiesPlace.org
www.netbullies.com
www.Peers2Peers.org
www.stopcyberbullying.org
www.teenangels.org
www.wiredkids.com
www.wiredsafety.org

WHO
Working to Halt Online Abuse

www.haltabuse.org

WHOA-KTD
Working to Halt Online Abuse Kids/Teen Division

www.haltabusektd.org

World Vision—Children in Crisis

Rienk van Velzen
Regional Communications Director
P.O. Box 28979
2084 Nicosia
Cyprus

PHONE: +31-180-525-747
FAX: +31-180-523-181
MOBILE: +31-6-5183-2040
E-MAIL: rienk_van_velzen@wvi.org

....

SITES AND RESOURCES FOR KIDS

100 Page Press

www.100pagepress.com

2 SMRT 4 U Campaign

www.2smrt4u.com

Children's Television Workshop

www.ctw.org

The Children's Internet

110 Ryan Industrial Court
Suite 9
San Ramon, CA 94583

PHONE: 1-925-743-9420
FAX: 1-925-743-9870
E-MAIL: info@tcimail.net

www.thechildrensinternet.com

Disney Daily Blast

www.disneyblast.com

The JASON Project

44983 Knoll Square
Ashburn, VA 20147

TOLL FREE: 1-888-527-6600
PHONE: 1-703-726-4232
FAX: 1-703-726-4222
E-MAIL: info@jason.org

www.jason.org

The National Crime Prevention Council Presents McGruff & Scruff and the Crime Dogs

15 West Strong Street
Pensacola, FL 32501

TOLL FREE: 1-800-915-4653
PHONE: 1-850-434-0500
FAX: 1-800-600-2505
E-MAIL: info@crimedog.com

www.crimedog.com

NetSmartz Workshop

National Center for Missing & Exploited Children

699 Prince Street
Alexandria, Virginia 22314-3175

PHONE: 1-703-274-3900
FAX: 1-703-274-2200

www.NetSmartz.org

PBS Online

www.pbs.org

See Appendix B for more kid-friendly websites.

GOVERNMENT AGENCIES/ LAW ENFORCEMENT/ LEGAL ORGANIZATIONS

American Center for Law and Justice

P.O. Box 90555
Washington, DC 20090-0555

TOLL FREE: 1-800-684-3110
LEGAL HELP LINE: 1-757-226-2489
LEGAL HELP FAX: 1-757-226-2836

www.aclj.org

CyberTipline National Center for Missing & Exploited Children

Charles B. Wang International Children's Building

699 Prince Street
Alexandria, Virginia 22314-3175
The United States of America

PHONE: 1-703-274-3900
FAX: 1-703-274-2200
24-HOUR HOTLINE: 1-800-THE-LOST
(1-800-843-5678)

www.cybertipline.com

The Cyber Law Enforcement Organization

Trenton Centre Post Office
P.O. Box 22073 Trenton
Ontario Canada K8V 6S3

CONTACT: Parry Aftab
PHONE: 1-201-463-8663
E-MAIL: parry@aftab.com

www.cyberlawenforcement.org

Federal Bureau of Investigation

J. Edgar Hoover Building
935 Pennsylvania Avenue, NW
Washington, DC 20535-0001

PHONE: 1-202-324-3000

www.fbi.gov

Interpol

200 Quai Charles de Gaulle
69006 Lyon
France

www.interpol.com

International Association of Chiefs of Police

515 N. Washington Street
Alexandria, VA 22314-2357

PHONE: 1-703-836-6767

www.theiacp.org

National Association of Chiefs of Police

3801 Biscayne Blvd.
Miami, FL 33137

PHONE: 1-305-573-0070

www.aphf.org

National Association of Police Organizations

317 South Patrick Street
Alexandria, VA 22314

PHONE: 1-703-549-0775
FAX: 1-703-684-0515

www.napo.org

National Criminal Justice Reference Service

Juvenile Justice Clearinghouse
P.O. Box 6000
Rockville, MD 20849-6000

TOLL FREE: 1-800-851-3420
FAX: 1-301-519-5600

www.ncjrs.org

Obscenity Crimes

www.obscenitycrimes.org

Office of Juvenile Justice and Delinquency Prevention (OJJDP)

810 Seventh Street, NW
Washington, DC 20531

PHONE: 1-202-307-5911

www.ojjdp.ncjrs.org/

Operation Blue Ridge Thunder

*Bedford County Sheriff's Office
Internet Crimes Against Children
Task Force*
Lieutenant Michael Harmony
Special Investigation Division

PHONE: 1-540-586-4800
www.blueridgethunder.com

Project Safe Childhood

U.S. Department of Justice
810 Seventh Street, NW
Washington, DC 20531

www.projectsafechildhood.org

United States Attorney General

950 Pennsylvania Avenue, NW
Washington, DC 20530-0001

PHONE: 202-514-2000

www.usdoj.gov/ag

U.S. Department of Education (DOE)

Office of Educational Research and Improvement

400 Maryland Ave., SW
Washington, DC 20202-0498

TOLL FREE: 1-800-USA-Learn
(1-800-872-5327)
(Spanish Speakers available)

TTY: 1-800-437-0833

PUBLICATION:
Parents Guide to the Internet

www.ed.gov

U.S. Department of Justice (DOJ)

950 Pennsylvania Avenue, NW
Washington, DC 20530-0001

MAIN PHONE: 1-202-514-2000
ATTORNEY GENERAL: 1-202-353-1555
E-MAIL: AskDOJ@usdoj.gov

www.usdoj.gov

U.S. Department of State

Trafficking in Persons Office
2201 C Street, NW
Washington, DC 20520

PHONE: 1-202-647-4000

www.state.gov

VIRGINIA RESOURCES

Virginia Attorney General's Office

Office of the Attorney General
900 East Main Street
Richmond, VA 23219

PHONE: 1-804-786-2071

www.oag.state.va.us

Virginia Parent Teacher Association (VAPTA)

1027 Wilmer Avenue
Richmond, VA 23227-2419

PHONE: 1-804-264-1234
FAX: 1-804-264-4014

www.vapta.org

Virginia Department of Education

P.O. Box 2120
Richmond, VA 23218

TOLL FREE: 1-800-292-3820

www.doe.virginia.gov

Virginia Association of Independent Schools

8001 Franklin Farms Drive
Richmond, VA 23229

PHONE: 1-804-282-3592

www.vais.org

Enough Is Enough Position on
SOCIAL NETWORKING SITES

Enough Is Enough (EIE) believes that children under the age of 18 are safest when they are not on social networking sites or online gaming sites; however, for children today, social networking has become a way of life. Social networking sites are virtual communities where people convene to chat, IM, post pictures, and blog. These sites also give children the opportunity to share stories, connect, and express themselves in new and often exciting ways. Kids choose screen names and fill out profiles containing information about their ages, hometown, schools, likes, and dislikes; friends post comments, take quizzes, rate each other, and can even give each other virtual gifts. As these sites continue to evolve, they offer new applications that allow kids to do all of the things they enjoy doing in the tangible world in a virtual world.

Despite the many positives of this new technology, law enforcement confirms that it is difficult to protect kids on these sites because it is nearly impossible to be certain with whom you are communicating. A child may become online "friends" with a disguised predator, or a peer may use the information included on a child's profile to harass them or post inappropriate content on another child's profile. Additionally, these sites often contain inappropriate content, language, and even pornography.

Parents must decide whether the benefit outweighs the risk regarding social networking sites. Before allowing children to use social networking sites, EIE encourages parents to familiarize themselves with the content and activities on the site and thoroughly review the safety practices and privacy tool features of the site in question.

If parents choose to allow their children on a social networking site, we recommend that parents set up their own profile and make sure you, as the parents, are added to your child's "friend list," because if their profile is set to private (as it should be!), you will not be able to view any of their information.

Many parents who allow their teens to use social networking sites have discovered that they can use the virtual community to monitor, interact with, and encourage their kids in a new and exciting way. By being added to their teen's "friend" list, parents can use these sites as a second pair of "eyes" and "ears" to help them understand their teen's online and offline world.[xix]

EIE encourages parents to diligently supervise their teen's social networking activities and implement **Rules 'N Tools®** *to keep their children safe on social networking sites.*

[xix] Illian, Jason. MySpace, MyKids. (Eugene OR: Harvest House publishers, 2007), p. 13.

A CONVICTED SEX OFFENDER SPEAKS OUT:

The Double Life of a Former School Teacher

In the spring of 2008, Enough Is Enough (EIE) President Donna Rice Hughes and a film crew interviewed convicted sex offender "John Doe" (JD) under the condition of anonymity. The interview was granted by the office of the Virginia Attorney General, and interview excerpts are included to educate parents about the modus operandi of Internet predators and to empower them to protect their children from victimization.

The former elementary teacher is serving out his sentence after pleading guilty to forcible sodomy, production of child pornography, and online solicitation of children. In the interview, John Doe revealed he was sexually abused as a child, a fate that one out of six boys endure before reaching adulthood.

During another interview, distinguished neuropsychiatrist, Dr. W. Dean Belnap, noted a disturbing trend echoed in numerous reports on pedophilia: pedophiles were commonly abused as children, ultimately perpetuating their sex offenses later in life.[xx] Jonathan Larcomb, who works in the Computer Crimes Section of the Office of the Attorney General (Va.), elaborated further as to the effect child pornography has on pedophiles' willingness to act on their desires, saying, "There's definitely research to indicate that child pornography fuels the desire and fuels the fire in someone who is interested sexually in children to go ahead and act on that."

It should be noted that *any* sexual offense committed against a child—no matter the severity of the offense or the life events that may have ultimately led up to the offense—is inexcusable and intolerable and a crime which should be prosecuted to the fullest extent of the law.

The following excerpts from the interview with John Doe have been included in this workbook in an effort to take parents inside the mind of a sexual predator in order to empower them to protect their children from becoming victimized from such individuals.

[xx] Dombrowski, S.C., J. W. LeMasney, C. E. Ahia, and S. A. Dickson. "Protecting children from online sexual predators: Technological, legal, and psychoeducational considerations." Professional Psychology: Research and Practice 35.1 (2004) 65-73.

The Role of Pornography

EIE: Do you think pornography played a role in some of the choices you made later in life?

"JD": Absolutely. I think that pornography absolutely played a role in those choices…seeing the pornography just sort of made sex very commonplace—it was not taboo. I didn't use pornography myself until I got the Internet. Initially it was heterosexual, mild pornography, and then there comes a point where it doesn't satisfy anymore, so I started looking at child pornography.

EIE: So you started with adult, heterosexual pornography, and [then] did you move right from that into child pornography?

"JD": When you're online there are pictures and e-mails sent often. Anytime you would go into a chat room, pictures are sent out, and pictures of child pornography would crop up amongst the other heterosexual pornography, and from that, I just continued to use the child pornography.

Grooming Techniques

"JD": As far back as I can remember, in my adult life, I always related well to kids…on their level…I would seek children as peers, instead of as an adult-child situation. What I would attempt to do would be to find out what their interests are and attempt to relate to their interests. The children that I related to were between 11 and 14. I originally went into chat rooms and from that point I would have instant message conversations. And it really started as a very typical conversation that two youth would have with each other on the playground. From that point the conversation would take on a more sexual tone. In a three-hour period of time online, I would probably talk to about 25 children.

 REMEMBER: Know your child's online activities and friends!

EIE: Did any of the kids you talked to confide in you about issues and problems that they had with their parents?

"JD": Certainly, a majority of the time that I spoke to children, they would have issues that they would share with me that were personal issues. I absolutely believe that the kids who I talked to, especially the ones that I spoke to most frequently, saw me as a friend. I'm certain that they trusted me. I'm certain that they liked me.

REMEMBER: **Teach your children to protect their personal information!** Intimate personal information should not be posted and should only be shared with a trusted personal friend that you and your child know offline!

EIE: Were kids willing to send sexual pictures?

"JD": Kids were very, very willing to send pictures of a sexual nature. It did not take a lot of convincing to get that type of picture.

EIE: In one of the articles, it said you had posed like a girl for other boys, how did you do that?

"JD": It would be my goal to find out what type of person it is that they were looking to speak to. So if it was a 13- or 14-year-old boy who was interested in speaking to a 13- or 14-year-old female, then I would be that female. There are millions of pictures online that you can download and send as far as this is who I am.

REMEMBER: You can NEVER detect a disguised predator!

EIE: What pushed you from conversations with children about sex to an actual encounter?

"JD:" I did have both an online and offline relationship with a student who I had taught prior to having any interaction with him outside of the classroom. There was no other interaction. However, I became close to

his family. As far as his parents, they had actually invited me to their house several times. We'd go to ball games or go to the circus or various things like that, and it was when that private time, that alone time, was so prevalent that the opportunity presented itself. At the time that the sexual interaction was taking place... I was 25. He was 14.

 REMEMBER: **Children who are sexually abused often know their offender** (30–40% of these victims are abused by a family member and 50% are abused by someone outside the family whom they know and trust.[xxi])

Double Life

EIE: Help us to understand how you would compartmentalize your role as a teacher and then have this kind of online interaction.

"JD": The Internet takes away most if not all inhibitions that people have and prior to that I never would have even considered having any type of interaction with a child. The adult person in me was say[ing]: "No. This cannot happen. You cannot do that." But the moment I got online, it made absolutely no difference. The Internet made it seem not only possible but acceptable and so I was very clearly two different people, I don't think there's anything that could have been done to stop me from getting online.

Words to Parents

"JD": The Internet is not the appropriate place for parents to give them their privacy. I don't believe that children have the available resources, the knowledge, and the wisdom, to be able to prevent a predator from approaching them. There is a good healthy amount of fear that the kids need to have, because I think they're very trusting. Children who do not have parents that are communicating with them or listening to them or have established a trust relationship with them would be most susceptible to that type of contact. Parents need to maintain consistent communication with a child, really whether the child wants it or not. And I think a child needs to feel safe in talking to their parent.

xxi United States. Dept. of Justice. Natl Institute of Justice. Youth Victimization: Prevalence and Implications. Apr. 2003. <http:// www.ncjrs.gov/pdffiles1/ nij/194972.pdf>.

APPENDIX B
INTERNET SAFETY RESOURCES

Disclaimer of Endorsement. Reference herein to any specific commercial products, process or service by trade name, trademark, manufacturer, or otherwise, does not necessarily constitute or imply its endorsement, recommendation, or favoring by Enough Is Enough. This document contains links to websites maintained by other public/private organizations. These links are for information purposes only and the presence of the link does not constitute an endorsement of the site or any posted material.

* Screen captures as of September 2008.

INTERNET FILTERING AND MONITORING SOFTWARE

Activity Logger:
www.softactivity.com

American Family Filter by BSecure
http://bsecure.com/offers/afafilter.aspx?13850

BeNetSafe:
www.benetsafe.com

Bsafe Online:
www.bsafeonline.com

Children's Internet:
www.thechildrensinternet.com

Clean Internet.com:
www.cleaninternet.com

Content Cleaner:
www.contentpurity.com

ContentProtect:
www.contentwatch.com

CyberPatrol:
www.cyberpatrol.com

Cyber Sentinel:
www.cybersentinel.com

CYBERsitter:
www.cybersitter.com

eBlaster:
www.spectorsoft.com

FamiLink:
www.familink.com

Family Cyber Alert:
www.itcompany.com

FilterGate:
www.filtergate.com

FilterPak:
www.surfguardian.net/products.shtml

Guardian Monitor:
www.guardiansoftware.com

IamBigBrother:
www.iambigbrother.com

IMSafer:
www.imsafer.com

Christian Net:
www.cnonline.net

iShield:
www.guardwareinc.com

K9 Web Protection:
www.k9webprotection.com

KidsNet:
www.kidsnet.com

McAfee Internet Security Suite:
http://us.mcafee.com

McGruff SafeGuard:
www.GoMcGruff.com

Microsoft Windows Live OneCare:
www.windowsonecare.com

Miss America Kid-Safe Web Browser:
www.missamericakids.com

NetIntelligence:
www.netintelligence.com

Netsweeper:
www.netsweeper.com

Netmop:
www.netmop.com

Net Nanny:
www.netnanny.com

Norton Internet Security:
www.symantec.com

Online Safety Shield:
www.onlinesafetyshield.com

Optenet PC:
www.optenetpc.com

Parental Control Bar:
www.wraac.org

PC Tattletale:
www.pctattletale.com

Razzul:
www.kidinnovation.com

SafeEyes:
www.internetsafety.com/safe-eyes

Sentry Parental Controls:
www.sentryparentalcontrols.com

Sentry Remote:
www.sentryparentalcontrols.com

SnoopStick:
www.snoopstick.com

Spector Pro:
www.spectorsoft.com

SpyAgent:
www.spytech-web.com/software.shtml

Surf On the Safe Side:
www.surfonthesafeside.com

SurfPass:
www.cogilab.com

Webroot Child Safe:
www.webroot.com

WebWatcherKids:
www.webwatcherkids.com

▲ NETNANNY

▲ BSAFEONLINE

▲ SYMANTEC

PARENTAL CONTROL WEBSITES

AOL:
http://parentalcontrols.aol.com

AT&T:
www.att.com/smartlimits
www.att.com/safety

Cablevision:
www.powertolearn.com/internet_smarts/index.shtml

Charter:
www.charter.com/Visitors/
NonProducts.aspx?NonProductItem=65

Comcast:
http://security/comcast.net

Cox:
www.cox.com/takecharge/internet_controls.asp

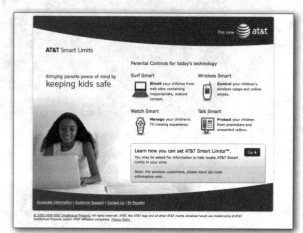

▲ AT&T

▲ AOL

Enough·Is·Enough
Making the Internet Safer for Children and Families

EarthLink:
www.earthlink.net/software

InsightBroadband:
www.insightbb.com/pcsecurity

NetZero:
www.netzero.net/support/security/tools/
parental-controls.html

Qwest:
www.incredibleinternet.com

Time Warner:
www.timewarnercable.com/centralny/products/
internet/parentalcontrols.html

Verizon:
netservices.verizon.net/portal/link/main/safety

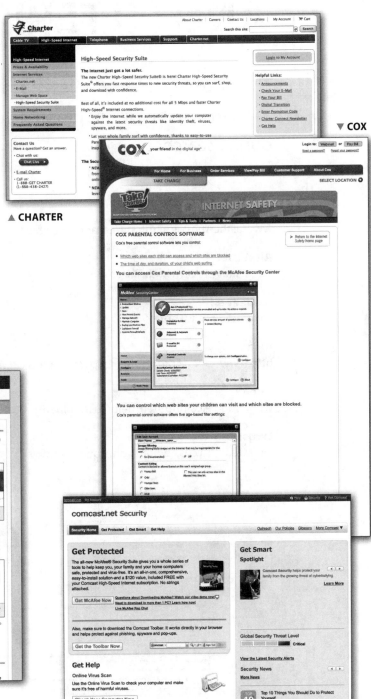

▲ CHARTER

▼ COX

▲ COMCAST

▲ VERIZON

SEARCH ENGINES AND FILTERING OPTIONS

The following are examples of search engines that offer filtering tools to help block inappropriate content that kids might stumble upon during searches:

AllTheWeb:
www.alltheweb.com/customize?backurl=Lw&withjs=1

AltaVista:
www.altavista.com/web/ffset?ref=/

AskJeeves:
www.ask.com/webprefs

Bing:
http://www.bing.com/settings.aspx?ru=%2f&FORM=SELH1

Google:
www.google.com/intl/en/help/customize.html#safe

Lycos:
www.search.lycos.com/adv.php?quer=&adf=

Yahoo:
www.myweb.yahoo.com

▼ BING

▼ GOOGLE

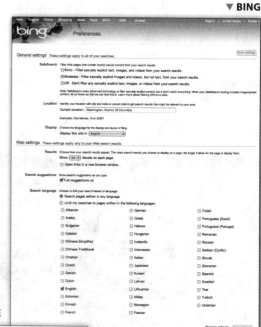

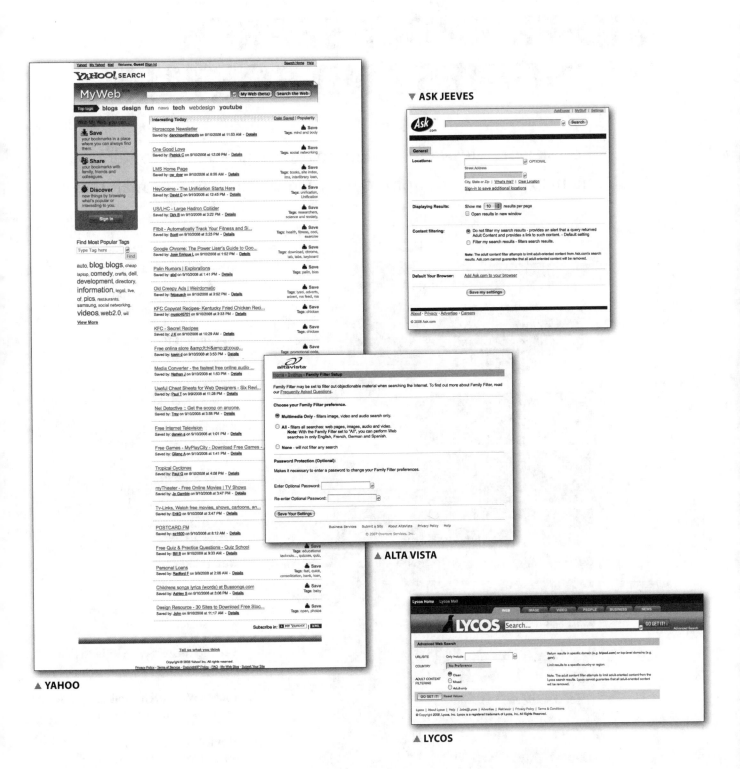

▲ YAHOO

▼ ASK JEEVES

▲ ALTA VISTA

▲ LYCOS

KID-FRIENDLY SEARCH ENGINES AND PORTALS

The following sites will allow kids to access kid-friendly content and help prevent kids from coming across inappropriate material:

▲ YAHOO! KIDS

AOL for Kids (U.S.):
www.kids.aol.com

AOL for Kids (Canada):
canada.aol.com/aolforkids

Ask Jeeves for Kids:
www.askkids.com

Dibdabdoo:
www.dibdabdoo.com

Education World:
www.education-world.com

Fact Monster:
www.factmonster.com

Kids.gov:
www.kids.gov

NetTrekker:
www.nettrekker.com

SearchEdu.com:
www.searchedu.com

Surfing the Net with Kids:
www.surfnetkids.com

TekMom's Search Tools for Students:
www.tekmom.com/search

ThinkQuest Library:
www.thinkquest.org/library

▼ FACT MONSTER

▲ AOL FOR KIDS

▲ THINKQUEST LIBRARY

▲ ASK JEEVES FOR KIDS

CHILD- AND TEEN-ORIENTED WEBSITES

Parents can also configure their web browsers to block access to web pages except for a few, select sites such as the following kid-friendly websites:

▼ **KABOOSE FUNSCHOOL**

◀ **THE CHILDREN'S INTERNET**

Clever Island:
www.cleverisland.com

Cybersmart Kids Online:
www.cybersmartkids.com.au

Disney Playhouse:
http://disney.go.com/playhouse/today

Disney's Club Blast:
www.disney.go.com/blast

Disney's Toon Disney Games:
http://psc.disney.go.com/abcnetworks/
toondisney/games

Disney Toontown Online:
play.toontown.com

JuniorNet:
www.juniornet.com

Kaboose Family Network:
www.kaboose.com

Kaboose FunSchool:
funschool.kaboose.com

KidsClick:
www.kidsclick.org

▲ PBS KIDS

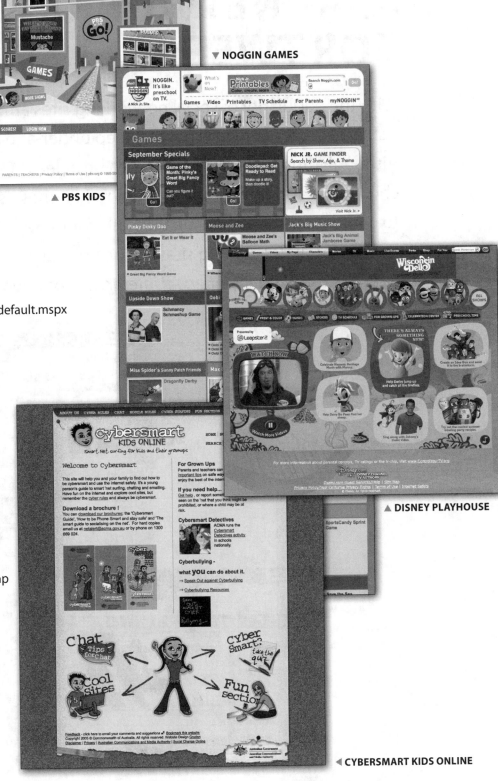

▼ NOGGIN GAMES

▲ DISNEY PLAYHOUSE

◄ CYBERSMART KIDS ONLINE

Kids First!:
www.kidsfirst.org

Microsoft At School:
www.microsoft.com/education/default.mspx

NetSmartz Kids:
www.netsmartzkids.org

Nickelodeon Games:
www.nick.com/games

Nick Jr. Games:
www.nickjr.com

Noggin Games:
www.noggin.com/games

PBS Kids:
www.pbskids.org/go

Safe Sites for Children (U.K.):
www.ssfchildren.co.uk/safety.php

Surfing the Net with Kids:
www.surfnetkids.com

The Children's Internet:
www.childrensinternet.com

Yahoo! Kids:
www.kids.yahoo.com

YoKidsYo:
www.yokidsyo.com

SOCIAL NETWORKING FOR TWEENS

With the popularity of social networking sites among youth, one of the issues of great concern is how to keep under-age users off of these sites. Although most sites require users to be at least 13 years of age, many children lie about their age in order to join these sites, risking exposure to content and activities suitable only for more mature teens. The following social networking sites are positive alternatives for tweens and younger users. (*Remember: All interactive communities can place your child at risk!*)

Club Penguin:
www.clubpenguin.com

Imbee:
www.imbee.com

Zoey's Room:
www.zoeysroom.com

▲ IMBEE

▼ **CLUB PENGUIN**

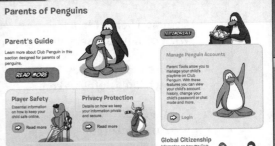

▼ **ZOEY'S ROOM**

VIDEO GAME INFORMATION

For video game reviews and information about the specific types of content kids will see or hear in a game, visit:

MediaWise "KidScore":
www.mediafamily.org/kidscore

Common Sense Media:
www.commonsensemedia.org/game-reviews

Children's Technology Review:
www.childrenssoftware.com

Gamer Dad:
www.gamerdad.com

What They Play:
www.whattheyplay.com

▶ **WHAT THEY PLAY**

▲ **CHILDREN'S TECHNOLOGY REVIEW**

ENOUGH·IS·ENOUGH
Making the Internet Safer for Children and Families

◄ COMMON SENSE MEDIA

▼ KIDSCORE

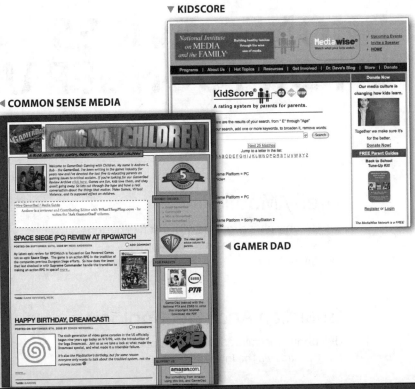

◄ GAMER DAD

ESRB
GAME RATING GUIDE

Early Childhood

Titles rated **EC (Early Childhood)** have content that may be suitable for ages three and older. Contains no material that parents would find inappropriate.

Everyone

Titles rated **E (Everyone)** have content that may be suitable for ages six and older. Titles in this category may contain minimal cartoon, fantasy, or mild violence and/or infrequent use of mild language.

Everyone 10+

Titles rated **E10+ (Everyone ten and older)** have content that may be suitable for ages ten and older. Titles in this category may contain more cartoon, fantasy or mild violence, mild language, and/or minimal suggestive themes.

Teen

Titles rated **T (Teen)** have content that may be suitable for ages 13 and older. Titles in this category may contain violence, suggestive themes, crude humor, minimal blood, simulated gambling, and/or infrequent use of strong language.

Mature

Titles rated **M (Mature)** have content that may be suitable for persons ages 17 and older. Titles in this category may contain intense violence, blood and gore, sexual content, and/or strong language.

Adults Only

Titles rated **AO (Adults Only)** have content that should only be played by persons 18 years and older. Titles in this category may include prolonged scenes of intense violence and/or graphic sexual content and nudity.

Rating Pending

Titles listed as **RP (Rating Pending)** have been submitted to the ESRB and are awaiting final rating. (This symbol appears only in advertising prior to a game's release.)

PHONE DEVICES FOR YOUNGER USERS*

Firefly Mobile—

a voice-only phone for kids with just five buttons. Two of the buttons are pre-programmed to call mom and dad.

Guardian Angel Technology—

GPS phone for children that allows parents to monitor their kids via the Internet.

Verizon Wireless's "Migo"—

has limited number of buttons for parents to program with approved and emergency-related numbers.

Wherify "Wherifone"—

offers robust GPS location tracking via the Internet. Restricts the downloading of games and text messages.

Tictalk—

lets parents enter phone numbers that can be called anytime and restrict numbers that can be called during certain times of the day.

*Thierer, Adam. Parental Controls & Online Child Protection: A Survey of Tools and Methods. The Progress & Freedom Foundation. 2008. <http://www.pff.org/parentalcontrols/Parental%20Controls%20&%20Online%20Child%20Protection%20%5BVERSION%203.0%5D.pdf>.

▲ TICTALK

▲ MIGO

▼ FIREFLY

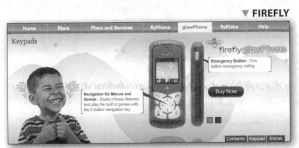

▲ GUARDIAN ANGEL

▲ WHERIFONE

TOP TEN TECHNICAL QUESTIONS
*What Every Parent Must Do**

FAUX PAW
The Techno Cat

10 TECHNICAL QUESTIONS
What Every Parent Must Do to Keep Children Safe Online

10 Common Questions About Internet Safety

Spyware, online fraud, and other Internet threats are certainly not new. But they are growing more sophisticated and criminal every day.

So how can you protect your children against these online dangers? And how can you provide a safe, appropriate Internet environment in the face of online criminals who know more about technology than you ever will?

Fortunately, there are good answers to these tough questions—thanks to a large, capable group of people and resources dedicated to helping you keep the Internet safe.
With only a little effort on your part, you can educate yourself...

Tap into the world's best resources for finding, monitoring, and defending your children against online threats....
And start using the Internet more safely and confidently.

Your part is straightforward.
• Just learn the right answers to these 10 common questions about Internet technology...
• Teach your children safe surfing practices...
• And take some easy steps to protect your computer.

1. How and why do I check the Web browser history?

2. How and why do I review temporary Internet files?

3. How and why do I remove spyware?

4. How and why do I scan for and remove viruses?

5. How and why do I use a firewall?

6. How do I monitor and block incoming files and information from the Internet?

7. How do I monitor and block outgoing files and information?

8. How do I adjust search engine settings (i.e. Google preferences)?

9. What safety and security tools are available on a typical home computer?

10. What are "updates" and why should I install them?

This parent resource is made possible through: 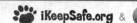 iKeepSafe.org & symantec.

10 TECHNICAL QUESTIONS
What Every Parent Must Do to Keep Children Safe Online

1. How and why do I check the Web browser history?

The Basics:
- The Web browser history lists the Web sites your child has visited recently.
- It's a useful resource for checking Internet activity.
- Web browser histories are easy to change and delete, so they are not foolproof.

To check the Web browser history in Internet Explorer, click the History icon.

This opens a History pane on the left side of your browser window that displays a list of recently visited sites.

You can click any item on the list for more detailed information.

You can also access additional browser history options by selecting Internet Options from the Tools menu.

 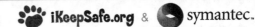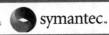

10 TECHNICAL QUESTIONS
What Every Parent Must Do to Keep Children Safe Online

Other browsers have similar browser history features that are generally very easy to access.

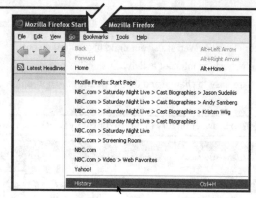

This parent resource is made possible through:  iKeepSafe.org & symantec.

Appendix B-20 | **Top Ten Technical Questions**

Copyright 2009 Enough Is Enough www.enough.org www.internetsafety101.org

10 TECHNICAL QUESTIONS
What Every Parent Must Do to Keep Children Safe Online

2. How and why do I review temporary Internet files?

The Basics:

- Your Web browser creates temporary files automatically to speed up your Internet experience.
- These files can include Web pages, images, sound files, or movies.
- Although the number and variety of temporary Internet files can be intimidating, examining them provides a very detailed view of exactly what your children have been viewing online.
- You should check temporary Internet files if there are unusual or suspicious holes in your child's browser history.
- Like the browser history, Internet-savvy children or teens can delete temporary Internet files fairly easily.

To view temporary Internet files in Internet Explorer, select Internet Options from the Tools menu.

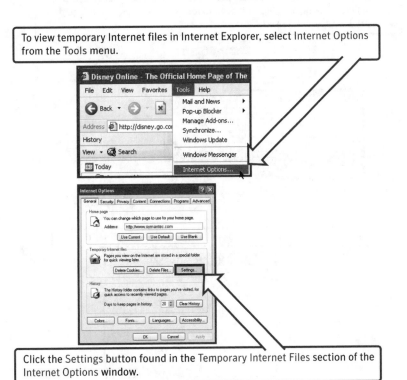

Click the Settings button found in the Temporary Internet Files section of the Internet Options window.

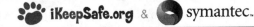

10 TECHNICAL QUESTIONS
What Every Parent Must Do to Keep Children Safe Online

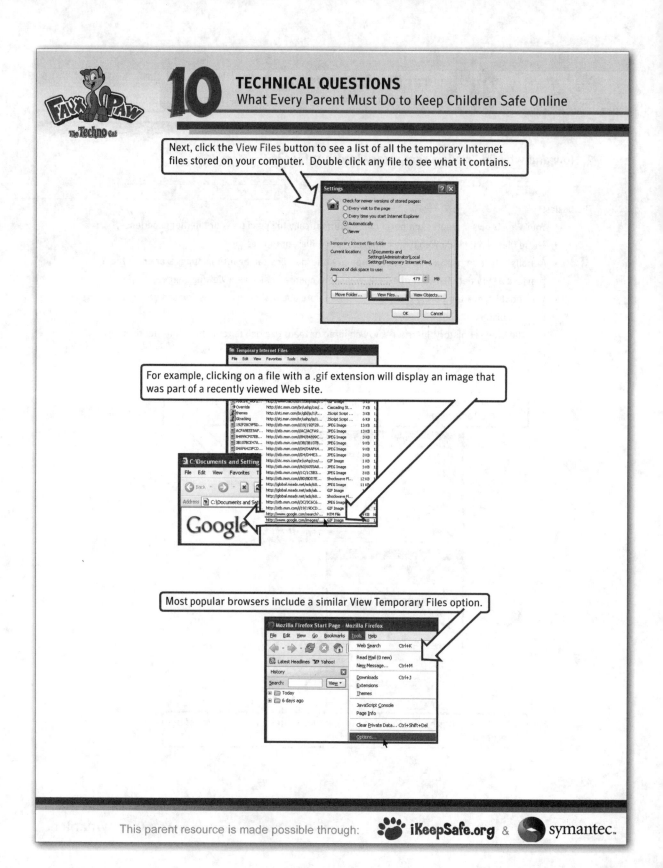

Next, click the View Files button to see a list of all the temporary Internet files stored on your computer. Double click any file to see what it contains.

For example, clicking on a file with a .gif extension will display an image that was part of a recently viewed Web site.

Most popular browsers include a similar View Temporary Files option.

10 TECHNICAL QUESTIONS
What Every Parent Must Do to Keep Children Safe Online

3. How and why do I remove spyware?

The Basics:
- Generally speaking, spyware is software that hides on your computer, tracks what you're doing online, and then sends that information over the Internet.
- Some types of spyware, called "keystroke loggers" actually record and send everything you type on your computer.
- Spyware software can sneak onto your computer when you download unsafe software and files—or even visit a hostile Web page.
- One major source of spyware is the peer-to-peer file sharing software commonly used to share music and videos online.

Tips for avoiding spyware and adware:
- Set concrete ground rules with your children. Specify exactly what they are allowed (and not allowed) to do online.
- Keep your PC in a public part of the house, where you can monitor your children's online activities.
- Avoid clicking on banner ads, links, or offers that appear too good to be true.
- Be cautious with file-sharing software and other potentially unwanted software.

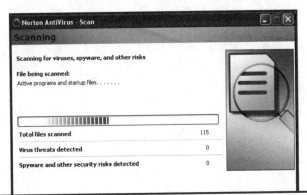

A quality Internet security program will scan your computer for spyware, adware, Trojan Horse programs, and other Internet risks...
And remove any malicious or unwanted software it finds.

 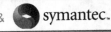

ENOUGH·IS·ENOUGH
Making the Internet Safer for Children and Families

10 TECHNICAL QUESTIONS
What Every Parent Must Do to Keep Children Safe Online

Many Internet security companies also offer free online scanning services to detect spyware, adware and malicious programs.

Click to scan your computer for Internet risks and threats right now.

This parent resource is made possible through:  iKeepSafe.org &  symantec.

TECHNICAL QUESTIONS
What Every Parent Must Do to Keep Children Safe Online

4. How and why do I scan for and remove viruses?

The Basics:

- Viruses are software programs that hide on your computer and cause mischief or damage.
- Viruses are also called worms, Trojan Horse programs, or other names, depending on how they behave. Together, all this malicious software is commonly referred to as "malware."
- Around 80% of malware today is designed to find and steal confidential information stored on your computer. This type of malware is sometimes called "crimeware."
- Malware can invade your machine through infected email attachments, "bots" that crawl the Internet looking for unprotected computers, and visits to "hostile" Web sites.

> Protecting your computer from malware isn't difficult. But it does require a quality antivirus or Internet security program.

> After you install your antivirus program, make sure the automatic protection feature is turned on. This will block malware the moment it attempts to creep onto your system.

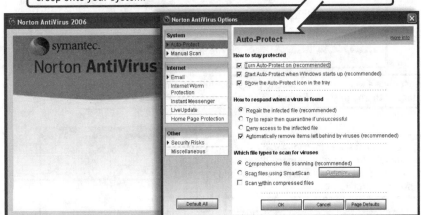

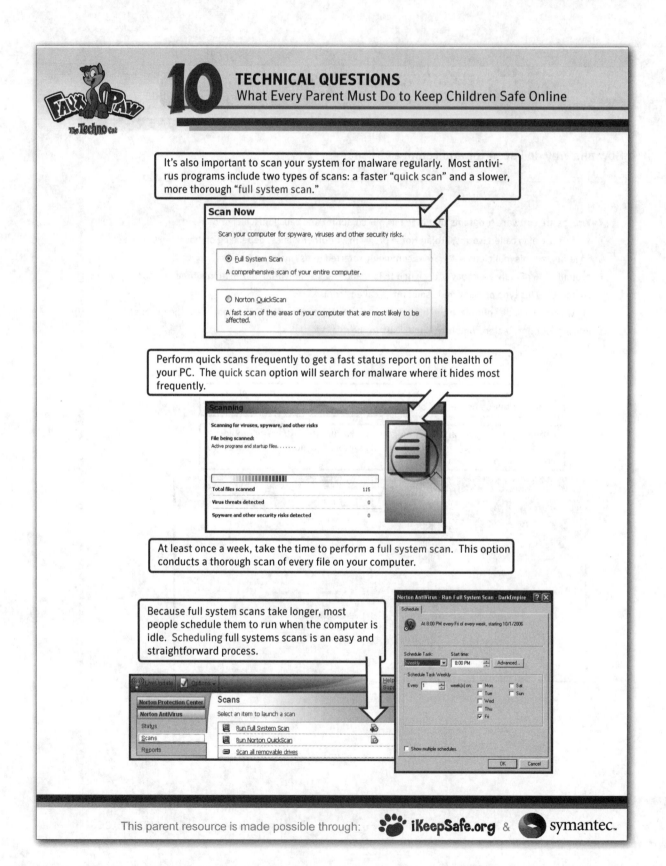

10 TECHNICAL QUESTIONS
What Every Parent Must Do to Keep Children Safe Online

It's also important to scan your system for malware regularly. Most antivirus programs include two types of scans: a faster "quick scan" and a slower, more thorough "full system scan."

Scan Now

Scan your computer for spyware, viruses and other security risks.

- ● Full System Scan
  A comprehensive scan of your entire computer.

- ○ Norton QuickScan
  A fast scan of the areas of your computer that are most likely to be affected.

Perform quick scans frequently to get a fast status report on the health of your PC. The quick scan option will search for malware where it hides most frequently.

Scanning

Scanning for viruses, spyware, and other risks

File being scanned:
Active programs and startup files. . . . . . .

Total files scanned	115
Virus threats detected	0
Spyware and other security risks detected	0

At least once a week, take the time to perform a full system scan. This option conducts a thorough scan of every file on your computer.

Because full system scans take longer, most people schedule them to run when the computer is idle. Scheduling full systems scans is an easy and straightforward process.

Norton AntiVirus - Run Full System Scan - DarkEmpire

Schedule

At 8:00 PM every Fri of every week, starting 10/1/2006

Schedule Task: Weekly   Start time: 8:00 PM   Advanced...

Schedule Task Weekly

Every 1 week(s) on: ☐ Mon ☐ Sat ☐ Tue ☐ Sun ☐ Wed ☐ Thu ☑ Fri

☐ Show multiple schedules.

OK   Cancel

Norton Protection Center
Norton AntiVirus
Status
Scans
Reports

Scans
Select an item to launch a scan

- Run Full System Scan
- Run Norton QuickScan
- Scan all removable drives

10 TECHNICAL QUESTIONS
What Every Parent Must Do to Keep Children Safe Online

It's also very important to keep your antivirus software up-to-date, since new malware is being released every day.

Most antivirus programs download updates automatically. Just make sure these updates are happening—and that your subscription stays current.

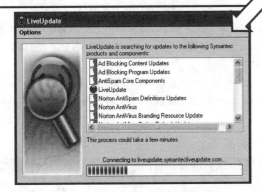

10 TECHNICAL QUESTIONS
What Every Parent Must Do to Keep Children Safe Online

5. How and why do I use a firewall?

The Basics:

- A firewall is your main line of defense against hackers, identity thieves, and other online predators.
- It monitors all the data flowing in and out of your computer—and automatically blocks harmful traffic.
- There are so many hackers looking for "fresh" unprotected machines that you should NEVER connect to the Internet without a firewall installed.
- Firewalls can be purchased separately—or as part of an Internet Security "suite" that typically includes firewall, antivirus, anti-spyware, anti-spam, and parental control software.

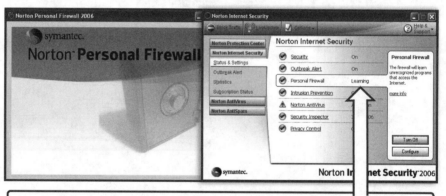

From the moment you install and activate your firewall software, it begins to "learn" about what programs you use online.

 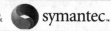

10 TECHNICAL QUESTIONS
What Every Parent Must Do to Keep Children Safe Online

As part of this process, you may receive occasional messages from the software asking you whether you would like to block, allow, or temporarily allow different programs to use your Internet connection.

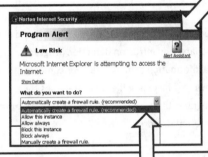

These questions will include advice from the software. In most cases, the best course of action is to simply follow the recommendation.

It's important to keep your firewall software current and up-to-date. Most firewalls download these updates automatically. Just make sure updates are taking place regularly—and that your subscription stays current.

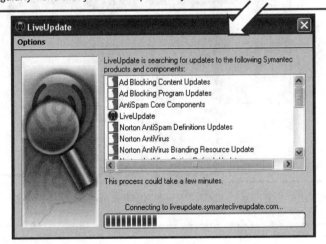

This parent resource is made possible through:  iKeepSafe.org & symantec.

10 TECHNICAL QUESTIONS
What Every Parent Must Do to Keep Children Safe Online

6. How do I monitor and block incoming files and information from the Internet?

The Basics:

- Three main types of security software can help you monitor and block harmful files from the Internet: firewalls, antivirus software, and intrusion detection programs.
- A firewall monitors the information coming into your computer for suspicious activity.
- Antivirus software "unwraps" incoming files and examines them for viruses, worms, and other threats.
- Intrusion detection programs block attacks that try to take advantage of security holes in common applications such as Internet Explorer.

For the most complete protection against dangerous incoming files, start by installing and activating a quality firewall program.

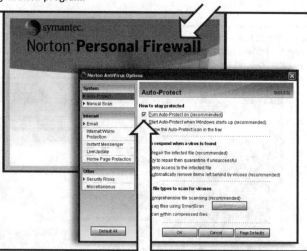

Next, make sure the AutoProtect feature in your antivirus program is turned on—and that your antivirus software is current and up-to-date.

 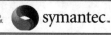

10 TECHNICAL QUESTIONS
What Every Parent Must Do to Keep Children Safe Online

Finally, install a program with intrusion prevention features to shield your computer from attackers who may try to take advantage of security flaws in Internet Explorer and other programs.

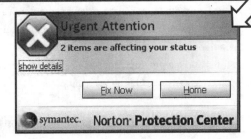

Many Internet security companies offer security "suites" that provide all of these capabilities in one easy-to-use, integrated package.

AntiVirus

Firewall

Parental Controls

AntiSpam

Privacy Controls

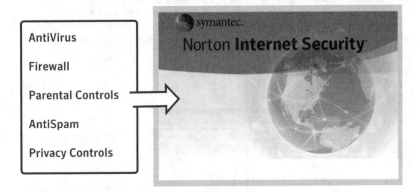

 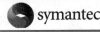

10 TECHNICAL QUESTIONS
What Every Parent Must Do to Keep Children Safe Online

7. How do I monitor and block outgoing files and information?

The Basics:

- It's very important to keep sensitive personal information from "leaking" onto the Internet.
- This can happen when personal information is sent from your computer over the Internet.
- Without proper precautions, people can use instant messaging programs to remove sensitive information from your computer.
- File-sharing or peer-to-peer networking programs such as Kazaa, Limewire, and Bit Torrent can also make it easier for people to access sensitive files on your computer.

To prevent people from accessing and removing sensitive information from your computer, start by installing a firewall program that alerts you whenever private information is about to be transmitted over the Internet.

Next, configure your instant messaging program to block anyone from downloading files from your computer.
In Yahoo Instant Messenger, select Preferences from the Messenger menu, select File Transfer from the list, and choose "Never allow others to download files from me."

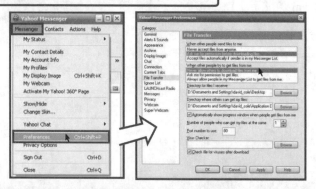

This parent resource is made possible through:  iKeepSafe.org & symantec.

ENOUGH·IS·ENOUGH
Making the Internet Safer for Children and Families

 TECHNICAL QUESTIONS
What Every Parent Must Do to Keep Children Safe Online

Other instant messaging programs have similar options—
usually found under the Preferences menu.

Finally, if you use a peer-to-peer file-sharing program, be sure to
specify one folder for exchanging files. Too many people accidentally
share their whole hard drive, which exposes all the files on your
machine to anyone using the same file-sharing program.

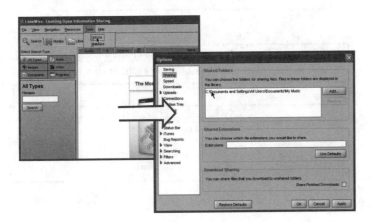

10 TECHNICAL QUESTIONS
What Every Parent Must Do to Keep Children Safe Online

8. How do I adjust search engine settings (i.e. Google preferences)?

The Basics:

- Search engines can provide children with fast, easy access to inappropriate material on the Internet.
- Most search engines allow you to block search results that are unsuitable for children.
- Blocking inappropriate search results greatly reduces the chance that your children will stumble across dangerous or objectionable material on the Internet.
- These search result filters are not foolproof—some unwanted content may still appear in the search results.

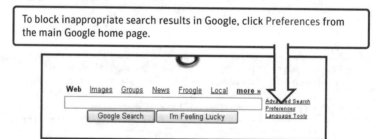

To block inappropriate search results in Google, click Preferences from the main Google home page.

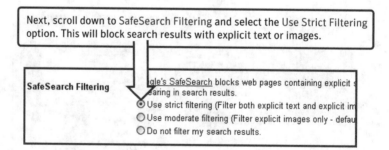

Next, scroll down to SafeSearch Filtering and select the Use Strict Filtering option. This will block search results with explicit text or images.

 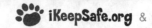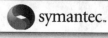

10 TECHNICAL QUESTIONS
What Every Parent Must Do to Keep Children Safe Online

Yahoo! and most other popular search engines offer a similar filtering function.

None of these filtering features are 100% accurate—and some unsuitable content may still slip through.
That's why it's important to teach your children to surf the Web safely—and take the time to explore the Internet with them.

This parent resource is made possible through:  & symantec.

10 **TECHNICAL QUESTIONS**
What Every Parent Must Do to Keep Children Safe Online

FAUX PAW
The Techno Cat

9. What safety and security tools are available on a typical home computer?

The Basics:

- Most home PCs run Microsoft Windows XP, which includes a number of important basic Internet security capabilities.
- The Windows Security Center provides important basic information about your computer's security status.
- Add-on Internet security products can offer more advanced, complete protection against Internet threats.

To access the Windows Security Center, open your Windows Control Panel and select Security Center.
The Security Center will tell you whether your antivirus and firewall programs are installed and working properly—and whether you are receiving automatic software updates.

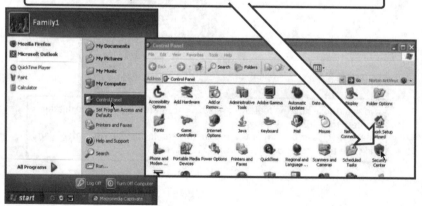

ENOUGH·IS·ENOUGH
Making the Internet Safer for Children and Families

10 TECHNICAL QUESTIONS
What Every Parent Must Do to Keep Children Safe Online

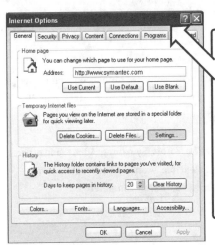

Microsoft Windows XP also includes an Internet Options control panel that allows you to manage important privacy settings.

This includes the ability to specify what types of cookies can be placed on your machine by different Web sites.

In many cases, cookies are harmless files that allow Web sites to remember your name or perform other useful functions.

But some cookies track your behavior online and can affect your privacy, so some level of control is advisable.

To change your Internet privacy settings, open your Windows Control Panel, select Internet Options, and click the Privacy tab.

 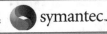

10 TECHNICAL QUESTIONS
What Every Parent Must Do to Keep Children Safe Online

10. What are "updates" and why should I install them?

The Basics:

- Updates—also called patches—are fixes or enhancements to the software running on your computer.
- Often, patches repair security "holes" in software that may be used by hackers to attack your PC.
- Other updates may keep your security software up-to-date with the latest information about new Internet threats.
- Updates are released regularly by software companies like Microsoft, Symantec, Adobe, and others.
- You should always apply updates as soon as they become available. Running the most up-to-date software makes it much more difficult for hackers to gain access to your computer.

> Microsoft software includes an "auto-update" feature that downloads and applies the latest software updates automatically.
>
> To activate auto-update in Microsoft Windows XP, open your Windows Control Panel and click Automatic Updates. Select the "Automatic" option to update your computer automatically.

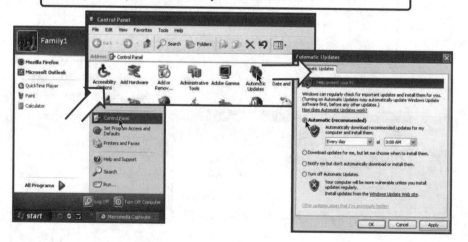

10 TECHNICAL QUESTIONS
What Every Parent Must Do to Keep Children Safe Online

Most security software also includes a feature that automatically downloads updates and information needed to detect and eliminate the latest viruses, worms, and other Internet threats.

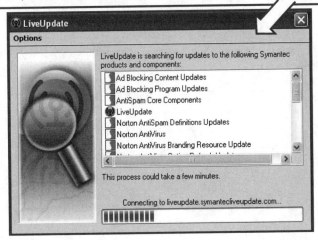

This parent resource is made possible through:  iKeepSafe.org & symantec.

10 TECHNICAL QUESTIONS
What Every Parent Must Do to Keep Children Safe Online

Keeping your family safe from online threats doesn't have to be difficult or intimidating.

Just become familiar with the answers to these questions...

Follow a few simple, common-sense rules...

And start using the world's leading Internet experts to protect your home PC against today's most sophisticated Internet threats.

This parent resource is made possible through:

APPENDIX C
PARTNER AND SPONSER INTERNET SAFETY MATERIAL*

INDUSTRY MATERIAL

NON-PROFIT MATERIAL

AOL PARENTAL CONTROLS

AOL ▶

AOL'S SITES FOR KIDS AND TEENS

RED

AOL's RED service has a completely new design for 2008! Every day on beRED.com, we're blogging about the latest celebrity news, music, movies, style, video games, college, and more. Teens can get in on the conversation by adding their own (moderated) comments and unique perspectives. Join the fun at **www.beRED.com!**

KOL

KOL.com is AOL's site for kids. On the site you will find Games, Movies, Music, Sports, Pets & Animals, TV, Cartoons, and Style areas. The site also includes kid-friendly email, weather and a My Web Favorites storage feature. Also, the site offers message boards that are monitored whenever they are open, and polls where kids can make their opinion heard. Kids can change the skin of their welcome screen to give it the look that they like best. KOL Jr. features games, stories and music for preschoolers to enjoy with mom or dad.

KOL.com and KOLJr.com are now free for everyone. So what are you waiting for? Head to **www.KOL.com** and start having fun!

More Resources On Online Safety

FBI—Parent's Guide to Internet Safety
www.fbi.gov/publications/pguide/pguidee.htm

ConnectSafely.org
www.connectsafely.org

Wired Safety
www.wiredsafety.org

Internet Keep Safe Coalition
www.ikeepsafe.org

GetNetWise
www.getnetwise.org

National Center for Missing and Exploited Children's CyberTipline
www.missingkids.com/cybertip

The NetSmartz Workshop
www.netsmartz.org

Enough Is Enough
www.enough.org

Pause Parent Play
www.pauseparentplay.org

WebWiseKids
www.webwisekids.org

Keep Your Children Safer On the Internet
AOL Keyword: **Parental Controls** • URL: **http://parentalcontrols.aol.com**

AOL PARENTAL CONTROLS

AOL PARENTAL CONTROLS: *Keep Your Children Safer On the Internet*

AOL has been the leader in family safety since pioneering parental controls in the early '90s. In August 2007, AOL launched the new Parental Controls product, which received a **4 out of 5-star review** from CNET's Download.com. With a redesigned landing page, streamlined registration path, and features frequently requested by parents, consumers will now find it easier to set up their master (parent) and sub (child) accounts, download the AOL Parental Controls software, and keep their kids safer online. And if you haven't heard already ... it's all **FREE**!

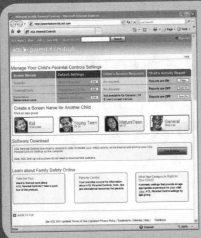

KEY FEATURES

Web Browsing Controls
You choose the content your child can view.

Email/IM Controls
You decide who can communicate with your child via email and instant messages.

Time Limits
You determine when and for how long your child can be online.

Activity Reports
You can receive email or Web reports of your child's online activity.

GETTING STARTED: *How do I set up AOL Parental Controls?*

Go to **http://parentalcontrols.aol.com** and in a few easy steps you can set up and customize an age-appropriate online experience for your child.

1 **Get a free AOL email address** (screen name)

2 **Set up an AOL.com email address** (screen name) **for your child(ren).** You can add up to six AOL screen names under your own, all for free, each with its own age-appropriate access level (kids-only, young teen, mature teen).

3 **Download and install the software** for AOL Parental Controls on each computer that your child will be using.

Once you're set up, you can easily customize the settings for each child at **http://parentalcontrols.aol.com.**

Keep Your Children Safer On the Internet
AOL Keyword: **Parental Controls** • URL: **http://parentalcontrols.aol.com**

AOL PARENTAL CONTROLS

AOL ▶

KEY FEATURES: *What features does AOL Parental Controls offer?*

Web Browsing Controls and Web Unlock

Web Browsing Controls give you the flexibility to decide which types of Web sites are appropriate for your child's age and maturity. No one knows your own kids better than you do. AOL Parental Controls allows you to choose which web sites your child can access.

Edit: Web Browsing | E-mails | IMs | Chat | Time Limits | Activity Reports | Downloads & Premium Services

Web Browsing Controls   Tell Me More

Allow your child to access:
All web sites, but block those known to contain adult or violent content ▾

Customize AOL's list of web sites your child is allowed to visit:
Allow a Specific Site | View Allowed Sites
Block a Specific Site | View Blocked Sites

Sorry, you don't have permission to view this web site.

http://www.cnn.com/

Ask For Permission   E-mail your parent to ask for permission

Get Access Now   Get access with your parent's permission now

Want to easily grant permission to view specific Web sites? With **Web Unlock**, your child can request access to specific Web sites that have been blocked by default for his/her age group.

IM and Chat Controls

IM Controls let you decide who can send your kids AOL Instant Messages (AIM). With **Chat Controls**, you can also limit them to visiting only AOL chat rooms. Our AOL hosts monitor all KOL message boards and remove any posts with inappropriate language or personal information.

Instant Message Controls   Tell Me More

Allow your child to IM with:
Only users I list ▾

Add a user to your allow list:
Allow a user | View allowed users

Block IMs that contain:
☑ Files, Images, Voice, Video, Hyperli

Chat Room Controls   Tell Me More

Do not allow your child to access:
☑ People Connection, AOL Auditorium & AIM Rooms
☐ Special Interest, RED & KOL Rooms
☐ Member-Created Rooms

Block chat rooms that contain:
☐ Hyperlinks

Email Controls

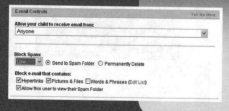

E-mail Controls   Tell Me More

Allow your child to receive email from:
Anyone ▾

Block Spam:
Low ▾ ⦿ Send to Spam Folder ○ Permanently Delete
Block e-mail that contains:
☑ Hyperlinks ☑ Pictures & Files ☐ Words & Phrases (Edit List)
☑ Allow this user to view their Spam Folder

Tired of your kids getting email from people they don't know? You can block mail from unknown or unwanted senders. AOL Mail helps put an end to the barrage of junk email messages and even filters out spam that may contain inappropriate content.

Keep Your Children Safer On the Internet
AOL Keyword: **Parental Controls** • URL: **http://parentalcontrols.aol.com**

AOL PARENTAL CONTROLS

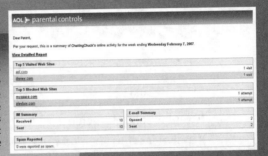

Activity Reports

Ever wondered exactly what your kids are doing while they're online? Of course you have. Thanks to **AOL Activity Reports**, you don't have to wonder anymore. Every time your kids go online with AOL, you can automatically receive an email report that lets you know where your child has been online. AOL also provides notification to the kids that their online activity is being monitored and a report will be sent to their parent or guardian.

Online Timer

How much time should your kids spend on the Internet? It's entirely up to you. With **Online Timer** you control the amount of time, the hours during the day or even days of the week that your kids can go online with AOL. Custom Daily Limits even allow you to select a different time limit for each day of the week.

SOFTWARE DOWNLOAD:
Why do I need to install it?

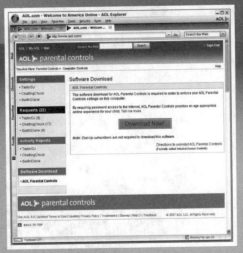

Software Download

The AOL Parental Controls software download is required, to enforce your existing **AOL Parental Controls** settings, monitor your child's Internet activity and provide you with the flexibility to decide which Internet sites and programs your child can use on a specific computer.

Go to http://parentalcontrols.aol.com **to download the software.** Please install the software on every computer that your child will be using to access the Internet.

Important Note: All users must sign-in to AOL Parental Controls before going online. Requiring password access to Internet-related programs reduces the risk of children encountering potential threats or inappropriate websites while online.

AOL Dial-up subscribers do not need to download this software. Parental Controls are automatically enforced when using an AOL dialup connection.

Keep Your Children Safer On the Internet
AOL Keyword: **Parental Controls** • URL: **http://parentalcontrols.aol.com**

at&t

Safe Surfing

You can rest easy knowing that your children are using the Internet safely with AT&T's Parental Controls.

Parental Controls include:

Permissions slips that allow your children to request access to unauthorized Web sites, and parents get to be the judge.

Tamper controls that alert you if your children attempt to change the settings.

Weekly report cards that detail your child's online activities including Mail and Internet surfing.

Manage your children's interaction with the Internet by setting limits on what they can see and do online:

Customize profiles for each family member to allow different usage limits.

Block access to specific services such as mail, messenger, chat groups, music and message boards.

Control access seven different ways: web filter, e-mail, instant messenger, online timer, permission slips and report card.

Manage master account and activate parental controls on up to 10 sub accounts.

Manage account settings from any Web connected computer.

AT&T Parental Controls package is free with AT&T high-speed Internet or dial-up service.

Visit **www.att.com/smartlimits** for more product details including cost & availability in your area.

at&t

ENOUGH·IS·ENOUGH
Making the Internet Safer for Children and Families

Safe Surfing

You'll know your children are safe with AT&T's Parental Controls, and signing up is simple.

How to create an account and activate Parental Controls:

1. Sign into the primary account.

2. Go to the Parental Controls page for your account.

3. Add sub accounts for each member of your family.

4. Create a username and password for each sub account.

5. Accept terms of service and privacy policies for the each sub account.

6. Select the configuration options you want for each sub account.

7. You'll be directed to a confirmation page for the account - begin setting up Parental Controls for the new user.

8. Verify the Parental Controls software is installed on your computer.

9. The first time you set access levels for an account, you'll be directed to a page with an "Activate" button. Click the "Activate" button.

10. Restart the computer to finish activating Parental Controls.

11. Activate Parental Controls for each computer used by your children.

Parental Controls offers four different access levels based on users' ages:

Kids (for children 12 and under): This is the most restrictive access level.

Teens (for children between 13 and 15): This access level gives older children more access to online services.

Mature Teens (for teens ages 16 and 17): This access level restricts only some types of Internet content.

Full Access (for adults): There are no restrictions on online use for this access level.

....

Each access level has different default restrictions for the following:

Web Filter: Controls what the user can access using an Internet browser.

Email: Controls whom the user can exchange email with.

Instant Messenger: Controls whom the user can exchange messages with.

Online Timer: Determines when and how long the user can be online.

Report Card: Provides the parent with reports on Internet access.

 at&t

Microsoft®

Get Game Smart

This PACT is made between _____ and _____ .
[Parent(s)/Caregiver(s)]   [Student]

Parental Involvement

We agree to make our home a safe, healthy and fun place to use media such as video games, TV and the Internet.

We will talk so that we understand the guidelines set out by _____ .
[Parent(s)/Caregiver(s)]

Access

_____ is permitted to go online: _____ With adult supervision _____ Without adult supervision
[Student]

Approval from a parent or caregiver **is / is not** required for accepting online friend requests.
[circle one]

Student's online profile(s) will be visible to: _____ Friends Only _____ Everyone _____ No One/Blocked

_____ is allowed to receive voice and text messages from: _____ Friends Only _____ Everyone _____ No One/Blocked
[Student]

_____ is allowed to use a Web camera with: _____ Friends Only _____ Everyone _____ No One/Blocked
[Student]

To control access, Family Settings/Parental Controls have been activated on all video game systems and computers in our home: ◯

Content

_____ is permitted to play video games and watch movies and TV shows with the following ratings:
[Student]

ESRB Game Ratings: eC E E10+ T M   MPAA Movie Ratings: G PG PG-13 R

TV Ratings: TV-Y TV-Y7 TV-G TV-PG TV-14 TV-MA   Ratings controls are set on all systems: ◯   Passwords are set on all systems: ◯

_____ is permitted to use video games, TV and/or Internet *IF* the following conditions are met (e.g., homework completed):
[Student]

_____
[Conditions to meet]

Time

_____ is permitted to use video games, TV and/or Internet _____ hours per day OR _____ hours per week.
[Student]   # of hours   # of hours

Timer settings have been turned on for all video game systems and computers in our home: ◯

PACT Agreement

Our family agrees to this PACT and commits to maintaining a healthy and balanced media environment in our home.

Parent/Caregiver Signature(s): _____ Date: _____

Student Signature: _____ Date: _____

For more information on Microsoft Xbox 360 Family Settings and Windows Vista Parental Controls, please visit www.**GetGameSmart**.com.

Checklist

☐ Talk as a family and set rules for access, content, time and Web safety.

☐ Set Family Settings on all video game systems, TVs and computers.

☐ Discuss what video games, TV shows and Web sites are off limits both at home and at friends' houses.

☐ Find out who your kids are playing video games and interacting with online.

☐ Visit **GetGameSmart**.com for more helpful tips and tools.

myspace™

Youth Safety
TIPS FOR TEENS

Don't say you're older than you are.

MySpace members must be 13 years of age or older. We take extra precautions to protect our younger members and we are not able to do so if you do not identify yourself as such. MySpace will delete users whom we find to be younger than 13, or those misrepresenting their age to access content or areas they should not.

MySpace is a public space.

Members shouldn't post anything they wouldn't want the world to know (e.g., phone number, address, IM screen name, or specific whereabouts). Don't post anything that would make it easy for a stranger to find you, such as your local hang out. It's always fun to post pictures but remember that what you might consider a harmless picture of you and your friends in your uniforms at a school football game, is actually a map telling a stranger exactly where you go to school.

Don't post anything that could embarrass you later or expose you to danger.

Please remember that MySpace is public and many people have access to what you post, including potential employers, colleges, your teachers, and peers at school that you might not even know. You shouldn't post photos or info you wouldn't want adults to see or people to know about you.

Protect your privacy.

Set your profile to private which lets only your friends view your profile. Users under the age of 16 are automatically assigned a private profile. Only accept friend invitations from people you know and trust.

People aren't always who they say they are.

Be careful about adding strangers to your friends list. It's fun to connect with new MySpace friends from all over the world, but avoid meeting people in person whom you do not fully know. Remember that you don't really know who is on the other end of an Internet connection.

myspace™

Harassment, hate speech, and inappropriate content should be reported.

If you encounter inappropriate behavior, inform your parents or a trusted adult and report it to MySpace or the authorities.

Don't get hooked by a phishing scam.

Phishing is a method used by fraudsters to try to get your personal information, such as your username and password, by pretending to be a site you trust. If you suddenly start receiving abnormal bulletins or messages from a friend, they might have been phished. Check with them before opening any files or clicking on any links. If you think you, or a friend, are a victim or phishing, change your password immediately.

Avoid in-person meetings.

Don't get together in person with someone you "meet" online unless you are certain of their actually identity. Talk it over with an adult first. Although it's still not risk-free, arrange any meetings in a public place and bring along friends, your parents, or a trusted adult.

Think before you post.

What's uploaded to the net can be downloaded by anyone and passed around or posted online pretty much forever. You shouldn't post photos or info you wouldn't want adults to see or people to know about you.

NET NANNY PARENTAL CONTROLS

How Does Net Nanny Work?

Net Nanny uses dynamic contextual analysis (in conjunction with URL lists) to filter Web content. As Web pages are requested, Net Nanny's dynamic analyzing engine has the ability to understand its context and filter appropriately. Net Nanny's state-of-the-art dynamic contextual filtering engine ensures that your family members won't be exposed to pornography and other offensive content.

Net Nanny is the most trusted family-oriented filter that can be used as configured right "out of the box" or you can customize the filter settings according to your personal preferences and needs.

Top Rated Parental Control Features & Benefits

Stylish and User-Friendly - Net Nanny offers a simple, easy to use set-up assistant to help parents determine what online activities (Web sites, chat, gaming and social networks) are appropriate based on their children's age.

Remote Management – Powerful Remote Management tools to help parents manage and maintain Internet policies from any Internet connection. Net Nanny has been enhanced to synchronize your settings almost instantly.

Predator and Cyberbully Alerts - Net Nanny's new Instant Message Monitor feature examines the content of Instant Messages and alerts parents to possible online predators, cyberbullies and other inappropriate contacts and comments made through popular Instant Messaging programs.

Social Networking Dashboard - Parents can easily access and view their children's Social Networking activities on commonly used sites like Facebook™, through Net Nanny's powerful new Social Networking Dashboard feature.

- ✓ **#1 Rated Internet Filter**
- ✓ **Secure Site Filtering**
- ✓ **Time Management**
- ✓ **IM Logging & Blocking**
- ✓ **Integration With Windows**
- ✓ **Automatic Updates**

- ✓ **Dynamic Content Analysis**
- ✓ **Remote Management**
- ✓ **Customized Block Page**
- ✓ **Game Management**
- ✓ **Multi-User Customization**
- ✓ **Free Support**

- ✓ **"Safe Search" Feature**
- ✓ **Remote Reporting**
- ✓ **E-mail Notifications**
- ✓ **Peer-to-Peer Management**
- ✓ **Multi-Language Support**

"It's the first time we have been able to totally relax while our children were on the Internet." - Nancy

#1 Rated Parental Control

PC Magazine Editors' Choice
- 2nd year running ★★★★☆

FAMILY SAFETY SOFTWARE for the Internet

w w w . n e t n a n n y . c o m

SMobile Parental Controls

Solution Elements Include:

- **Monitoring Dashboard:** Log in to a web-based interface to view all monitoring and reporting data

- **E-Mail Monitoring:** Monitor e-mail messages sent and received from the child's mobile device

- **SMS/MMS:** View all transmitted and received SMS and MMS text messages

- **Location Tracking:** Easily locate and track the child and their device

- **Picture Monitoring:** View photos taken, sent and received by the device

- **Automated Alerts:** Parents are proactively notified via e-mail of inappropriate content or communication

- **Voice Communication:** Check call logs of all voice conversations conducted by the device

- **Anti-Theft:** From the dashboard, issue commands to remotely lock, wipe, or backup the device

- **Communication Control:** Block voice and SMS communication from unwanted sources

- **Application Monitoring:** view all third party applications currently installed on the child's mobile device

- **Contacts:** Gain insight into exactly who your child is communicating

- **Anti-Malware and Anti-Spam protection:** Protection from Spyware, Viruses, Trojans and Worms

"For just about every category of mobile media activity, if you look at the 13 to 17-year-old bracket they're doing more things with their phones than the average phone user... The same can be said for tweens - the 8 to 12-year-old crowd."

"47 percent of teenagers take photos with their mobile device - that's twice the industry average." - Source: M:Metrics, Inc

US teens sent and received an average of 2,272 text messages a month in the fourth quarter of 2008. - Source: The New York Times, 2009

Without question, cell phones have replaced PC's as the primary means that young people use to communicate. Whether it's surfing the Internet, or texting and e-mailing messages, the opportunity to have inappropriate communication, view improper content and pictures, or fall victim to exploitation has increased dramatically. Couple these threats with the increased mobility that cell phones provide and parents can find themselves completely unaware of the unsavory situations in which their children are being placed. Numerous media accounts have documented cases of online bullying, harassment and predatory sexual advances, while articles have shown examples of children sending inappropriate pictures of themselves to peers via their mobile phones.

SMobile Parental Controls give parents the necessary insight and control into the mobile activities of their children, while also protecting their devices from loss, theft, viruses and spyware.

Children demand the latest and greatest technologies and now parents can take the appropriate steps to secure their child's online mobile experience.

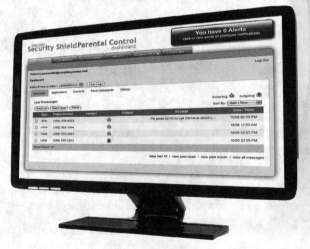

 symbian   RIM

4320 E. 5th Avenue • Columbus, OH 43219 • phone: 1-866-323-0480 • fax:614-251-4083 • **www.smobilesystems.com**

Parental control software is a great start to ensuring your child's experiences browsing the Web are safe and secure. The Verizon Parental Control service, which is also offered as part of the complete Verizon Internet Security Suite, can help you identify and block web sites you decide are inappropriate for your children.

Verizon Wireless Content Filters

By using Content Filters, account holders may allow their children to access content available through their Verizon Wireless handsets, including content accessible through Mobile Web 2.0, short code-based messaging campaigns, V CAST Music and V CAST Video, with confidence that the content will be age-appropriate.

Only Verizon Wireless offers age-appropriate content filters, which are easy to change as your child matures, and always free of charge:

 Content recommended for ages 7 and older. Includes content similar to TV-G, G-rated movies and no explicit rated songs.

 Content recommended for ages 13 and older. Similar to TV-PG/TV-14, PG 13 rated movies and no explicit rated songs.

 Content recommended for ages 17 and older. May include content similar to TV-MA, R-rated movies and explicit rated songs.

To learn more, please visit:

verizonwireless.com/parentalcontrols

Verizon Wireless Usage Controls

Usage Controls provide you with the tools to manage your family's budget and cell phone usage by allowing you to:

 Set voice and messaging allowances and receive free text alerts when your family member nears or reaches the allowance.

 Designate specific times of the day when your family member is not permitted to use messaging or data on his or her cell phone.

 Create lists of blocked phone numbers to prevent unwanted calls and text messages from being sent or received.

 Designate trusted numbers that can always communicate with your family member, regardless of other Usage Controls that are set.

 Create profiles and customize settings for each family member or each line on your account.

You can access and manage all the lines on your account online via My Verizon. To learn more, please visit:

verizonwireless.com/usagecontrols

It's Easier to Stay Connected with Family Locator from Verizon Wireless

Busy families with changing schedules and safety concerns need ways to stay connected and safe.

Verizon Family Locator, now available from Verizon Wireless, helps them do that and more.

 Locate your family:
Peace of mind is at your fingertips. Securely locate your family members' locations from your Verizon Wireless Device or the web.

 Receive arrival & departure updates:
Receive updates when your family members leave or arrive at locations that you define such as school, soccer practice or home.

 Set scheduled updates:
Choose times you want to verify whether a family member is inside or outside of a location you defined.

 Send text and place messages:
With integrated messaging capability, you can easily send text and place messages to your family members after locating them.

Learn more: **www.verizonwireless.com/familylocator**
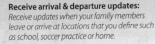

Verizon FiOS TV Parental Controls

Verizon FiOS TV offers a wide variety of programming for audiences of all ages. Some households may wish to block unsuitable or objectionable content.

FiOS TV Parental Controls make it easy to ensure that viewable programming is appropriate for all family members.

The controls allow you to:

- Manage what can and cannot be watched with a 4-digit PIN

- Control content using TV and MPAA ratings for shows and movies

- Control games using ESRB ratings

- Block all programming on specific channels individually

- Hide information for adult-rated content in TV listings and throughout the Interactive Media Guide (IMG)

- Prevent all unauthorized On Demand, Pay Per View, Gaming, and subscription purchases on your account

- Block promotional Video On Demand trailers

With just a few clicks of the remote, FiOS TV Parental Controls enable you to easily manage the content that comes into your home and make better decisions about what your children watch.

To learn more, please visit:

verizon.com/fiostvhelp

Verizon Online Parental Controls

Parental control software is a great start to ensuring your child's experiences browsing the Web are safe and secure. The Verizon Parental Control service from Verizon Online can help you identify and block Web sites you decide are inappropriate for your children.

The Parental Controls service allows you to:

- Block Web sites by categories

- Block or allow Web sites based on the URL of the site

- Block Internet access for certain programs or groups of programs

- Schedule when Internet access is available

Included with your Verizon Parental Controls service is the Verizon Security Advisor™, a FREE security test to see if your PC is protecting you from the latest online threats.

In addition to the free parental controls service, the Verizon Internet Security Suite also offers a package of Anti-Spyware, Anti-Virus, Firewall, Pop-up & Ad blocker, Privacy Manager, Fraud Protection and PC Tune-Up on multiple PCs for one low price.

To learn more and download free software, please visit :

verizon.net/parentalcontrol

PEACE OF MIND FOR
FAMILIES ONLINE

Meet *Faux Paw, the Web-surfing Techno Cat*, who teaches young children the safe and responsible use of technology through stories developed in collaboration with child psychologists, educators and law enforcement. The *Series* (books and animated DVDs) includes:

NEW FROM IKEEPSAFE...

Faux Paw Goes to the Games:
Balancing Real Life with Screen Time
shows children what can happen when
online games interfere with real-life goals.

Faux Paw's Adventures in the Internet teaches kids the basics of Internet safety: how to keep personal information safe, to keep away from Internet strangers, and to go to an adult for help when they see anything online that makes them uncomfortable.

iKeepSafe has a complete
line of Internet safety
products:

- *Faux Paw®* Books & DVDs
for ages 5-10

- **Curricula for educators**

- **Middle and high school
presentations**

- **Parent tutorials**

- **Group presentation
materials**

- *Parent Resource Center* at
www.ikeepsafe.org/PRC

- **Online videos & games**

Faux Paw Meets the First Lady:
How to Handle Cyber-bullying,
featuring First Lady Laura Bush,
teaches kids how to avoid online
harassment and, when necessary,
how to handle it.

- **Fun Stuff:**
  ➤ **Mousepads**
  ➤ **Pencils**
  ➤ **Posters**
  ➤ **Bookmarks**
  ➤ **Keytags**

AND COMING FALL 2008...

Faux Paw's Dangerous Download
shows children the security and
ethical risks inherent in peer-to-
peer downloading and encourages
them to download from reputable,
legal Web sites.

Available at
www.ikeepsafe.org

iKeepSafe, 4607 – 40th Street North, Arlington, VA 22207   info@ikeepsafe.org   703.536.1637   © 2008 All Rights Reserved

WEBWISEKIDS
WISDOM BEGINS WITH YOU

Make Web Wise Kids' programs part of your Community Shield Approach

*and use interactive computer games, not a lecture, to reach
today's youth with the message of safety*

WWK's programs for middle-school, high-school students and parents have proven extremely
effective in changing children's online behaviors. They address issues such as:

	**ONLINE LURING… PREDATORS… CHAT ROOMS…** *Missing* tells the story of Zack, a kid in Vancouver who forms an online friendship with Fantasma. This guy is so cool – he has an online magazine about beach life in California, and he sends Zack great stuff, like graphic arts and software. Little does Zack know that he is a predator. After they disappear into San Diego together, players work with a detective to rescue Zack and arrest Fantasma.
	**CYBERSTALKING… MODELING SCAMS… SPYWARE…** *Mirror Image* tells the story of teenagers Sheena and Megan, best friends who end up being victimized by a criminal. The lures of modeling and of online romance hook them both. Neither of the girls realizes that hacking software has been placed on their computers during their conversations with their "online boyfriends." Players work with a detective to track the predator and arrest him.
	**PIRACY… BULLYING… ILLEGAL DOWNLOADING…** *Air Dogs* was designed to show teenagers that online crimes have lifelong legal and social consequences for teens and their families. In the game, Luke is a teenager who shows great promise as a snowboarder. He needs money for gear and training, so he begins to counterfeit software in his basement. Players collect data and evidence to catch Luke's boss. The message of Air Dogs is clear: theft and extortion are crimes, whether you're 16 or 60.
	**Safety Tips… Web Site Danger Zones… Solutions** *Wired With Wisdom* has been uniquely designed to provide parents, teachers, law enforcement officers & youth leaders with useful information and solutions related to the problems that today's e-generation faces. The program is comprehensive without being complex, and the format is attractive and easy to navigate so that even the least Internet-savvy adult can enjoy learning. The subject matter is broken down into five segments: • Overall tips for Internet Safety • E-mail Safety Tips • Safety Tips for Social Networking • World Wide Web Safety Considerations • Cell Phone Safety

P.O. Box 27203, Santa Ana, CA 92799 * Tel. (714) 435-2885 * Fax 714-435-0523
www.webwisekids.org

NetSmartz.org

NetSmartz® Workshop

EDUCATE. ENGAGE. EMPOWER.

helping prevent
the victimization of children
online and in the real world

LEARN MORE

Get Involved

- Law-enforcement entities can present NetSmartz materials to the public as part of their outreach efforts

- State offices, attorneys general, and local and district school boards can partner with NetSmartz to make the program a part of their schools and communities

- Sponsorship from private corporations enables the NetSmartz Workshop and its innovative content to be shared globally via the Internet

NetSmartz® Workshop
National Center for Missing & Exploited Children®

Charles B. Wang International
Children's Building
699 Prince Street
Alexandria, VA 22314-3175
U.S.A.

1-800-THE-LOST®
(1-800-843-5678)
NetSmartz_contact@ncmec.org

EDUCATE

ENGAGE

EMPOWER

NetSmartz® Workshop

The NetSmartz Workshop is an interactive, educational safety resource from the National Center for Missing & Exploited Children® (NCMEC) that creates age-appropriate activities to help teach children how to be safer while online and in the real world.

- The program is designed for students in elementary, middle, and high school

- Parents and guardians, educators, and law enforcement can learn dynamic ways to teach safety

- On- and offline activities such as animated videos, real-life stories, and corresponding activity cards provide a learning experience for children to enjoy and relate to their daily lives

NetSmartzKids™

Clicky, Nettie, and Webster, animated characters, teach children how to recognize and avoid on- and offline dangers using interactive games, activities, and music.

NSTeens™

Issues such as social networking, cyberbullying, and gaming are addressed through comic-book-style characters who model safer practices.

Real-Life Stories

Materials focus on real-life stories shared by actual teens who have experienced victimization firsthand. These powerful stories teach teens to examine their behavior and encourage them to be proactive in preventing victimization of themselves and others.

The Goal

The goal of the NetSmartz Workshop is to extend the safety awareness of children and empower them with the knowledge to make safer choices on the Internet and in the real world. This is accomplished by

- Enhancing the ability of children to recognize and avoid dangers

- Helping children understand people they first "meet" on the Internet should never be considered their friend

- Encouraging children to report victimization to a trusted adult

- Promoting communication between adults and children about personal safety

Internet Safety Helpdesk & Hotline   1-888-NETS411

NetSmartz411 is a premier helpdesk and hotline for answering your questions about Internet safety, computers, and the Web. Parents, guardians, grandparents, teachers – any concerned adults - are welcome to use NetSmartz411 to better understand the opportunities and challenges children may face online.

At NetSmartz411.org, you can find answers to your questions about the online world! View the library for information ranging from social networking, instant messaging, cell phones, chatrooms, e-mail, and gaming. You will learn the potential risks to children and how to protect them. New Internet safety issues are addressed as they emerge so you will be getting the most current information available to help you protect this highly connected generation of children and teens.

Click on the "Ask an Expert" tab or call 1-888-NETS411 (638-7411) to ask a new question. Your questions will be answered by professionals who know a lot about Internet safety – the real-life analysts at the National Center for Missing & Exploited Children.

Get Started
- Go to www.NetSmartz411.org
- Review the top ten questions in the blue box to learn about the most current issues
- Type a phrase or keyword in the search box to learn more about a specific issue
- Click on the "Library" tab at the top
- Review the categories listed and click on one you want to learn more about
- Click on a sub-category to filter the information provided
- Click on a question to read the answer
- Click on the "Ask an Expert" tab at the top
- Fill in the required fields, including a question relating to Internet safety, computers, or the Web
- If you provide your e-mail address, you will automatically receive an e-mail with the number your request has been assigned
- An analyst will respond to your question by phone or e-mail within one business day
- Check back at NetSmartz411.org for new information and more current issues

NetSmartz411 is provided at no cost to the public by the National Center for Missing & Exploited Children. This service is made possible by generous donations from the Qwest Foundation.

TechMission
SafeFamilies
KEEPING CHILDREN SAFE ONLINE

TechMission provides free Internet Filtering Software and Parental Controls to help protect children online. This software represents a long awaited update building on We-Blocker, the most widely used FREE Internet filtering software which has had hundreds of thousands of downloads. The update includes:

- Adding over 300,000 sites to the blocked sites list

- Providing the ability to disable the splash screen

- Integrating extensive Webcast training for parents to protect their children online

- Improved graphics

We-Blocker's key features include the ability to:

- Block specific key words

- Set up multiple users at varying levels of access

- Review all websites visited

- Tailor filtering based on broad categories

To download the software, go to www.safefamilies.org/download.php.

NOTE: Do NOT install We-Blocker if you are running Windows Vista.

We realize that just having software is not enough. Parents and other care takers need to be trained on all strategies for protecting their kids online. Safe Families provides extensive online safety information on its website (www.safefamilies.org) in webcasts, videos, and downloadable documents. Additionally, a 50-page Free Online Safety Training & Manual is available at www.safefamilies.org/docs/manual.doc.

HOW TO REPORT A CYBER CRIME

TO REPORT A CYBER CRIME, PLEASE FILL OUT THE CYBERTIPLINE FORM OR CALL THE CYBERTIPLINE (both services are provided by the National Center for Missing and Exploited Children).

You will find this form at:
www.cybertipline.com

Or call:
1-800-THE-LOST.

TO REPORT INCIDENCES OF HARDCORE PORNOGRAPHY ONLINE:
www.obscenitycrimes.org

CONTACTING YOUR ELECTED OFFICIALS

Remember: As a voter and a constituent, you have the power to effect change and to protect children from online exploitation. Encourage your elected officials to be proactive about online safety by enforcing existing laws and supporting new laws needed to better protect children on the Internet! To find and contact your federal, state, and local officials, please visit:

www.usa.gov/Contact/Elected.shtml

HOW TO CONTACT ENOUGH IS ENOUGH

Thank you for your interest in and continued support of Enough Is Enough. Please feel free to contact EIE:

BY MAIL:
Enough Is Enough
746 Walker Road, Suite 116
Great Falls, VA 22066

www.enough.org
www.InternetSafety101.org

BY PHONE:
Office:
Local: 703-476-7890
Toll Free: 888-744-0004
Fax: 703-620-8889

BY E-MAIL:
info@enough.org
www.enough.org

DISCLAIMERS AND LEGAL NOTICES

1. NO WARRANTIES. USE OF THE *INTERNET SAFETY 101™* WORKBOOK AND CONTENT IS AT YOUR SOLE RISK. ENOUGH IS ENOUGH AND THE *INTERNET SAFETY 101™* WORKBOOK EXPRESSLY DISCLAIM ALL WARRANTIES OF ANY KIND, WHETHER EXPRESS OR IMPLIED, INCLUDING, BUT NOT LIMITED TO THE IMPLIED WARRANTIES OF MERCHANTABILITY, FITNESS FOR A PARTICULAR PURPOSE AND NON-INFRINGEMENT. Void where prohibited by law.

2. LIMITATION OF LIABILITY. You expressly understand and agree that Enough Is Enough and the *Internet Safety 101™* Workbook shall not be liable for any direct, indirect, incidental, special, consequential or exemplary damages, including but not limited to, damages for loss of profits, goodwill, use, data or other intangible losses (even if Enough Is Enough and the *Internet Safety 101™* Workbook have been advised of the possibility of such damages), resulting from:

(i) the use or the inability to use the *Internet Safety 101™* Workbook;

(ii) the cost of procurement of substitute goods and services resulting from any goods, data, information or services purchased or obtained from Enough Is Enough; or

(iii) any other matter relating to the *Internet Safety 101™* Workbook.

3. DISCLAIMER OF ENDORSEMENT. Reference herein to any specific commercial products, process, or service by trade name, trademark, manufacturer, or otherwise, does not necessarily constitute or imply its endorsement, recommendation, or favoring by Enough Is Enough. The views and opinions expressed herein do not necessarily state or reflect those of Enough Is Enough, and shall not be used for advertising or product endorsement purposes. This document contains links to websites maintained by other public/private organizations. These links are for information purposes only and the presence of the link does not constitute an endorsement of the site or any posted material. Although every reasonable effort has been made to present current and accurate information, Internet content appears, disappears, and changes over time. Please let us know about any existing external links that might be inaccurate or inappropriate.